# GO ➤

# NEXT

## THE MASTER KEYS TO MOVE FROM WHERE YOU ARE TO WHERE YOU ARE CALLED TO BE IN LIFE, BUSINESS, AND RELATIONSHIPS.

## TORREY MONTGOMERY

# GO NEXT

*Helping You Shift From Your Now To Your Next In Life, Business & Relationships*

## By

## Torrey Montgomery

### Copyright 2021 ICHAMPION Publishing

Published by iCHAMPION Publishing

P.O. Box 2352 Frisco, TX 75034

Content edit by Nikia Hammonds-Blakely and iCHAMPION Publishing

Library of Congress Cataloging-in-Publication Data Publisher and Printing by iCHAMPION Publishing

Written By: Torrey Montgomery
Cover Design By: iCHAMPION Publishing

ISBN: 978-1-7362684-9-0

Self-Help

Personal Development

# ACKNOWLEDGEMENTS

I would like to take this time to give a very special thank you to my wife Janelle Montgomery for your unending support of push into greatness. You have inspired me and encouraged me beyond my ability to articulate. You are amazing and I Thank God for everything that you are to me. I must also send a special shout out to my kids. Jasmine, Torrion, Tae Li, and Jyden. You all have inspired me each in a unique way.

To my dad Reverend Jackie Brooks. We miss you and everything that you were to our family. You poured into us, and we are seeing the harvest of the seeds that you sowed into our lives.

To my mom. You are my greatest supporter hands down. Thank you for the wisdom and consistency. Thank you for always encouraging and pushing me to be great.

To my sister I thank you for always being there for every season of my life. You have been a major piece to my journey and destiny.

To Bishop Gary McIntosh. Thank you for being a constant in my life. Your counsel and encouragement have been a lifeline to me.

To everyone that has supported, encouraged, allowed me to preach, minister, keynote, coach, inspire and be a voice to you, thank you for trusting me to serve you with the gift of God that is in me.

## TABLE OF CONTENTS

# INTRODUCTION

A s I sit here writing, my mind reflects on a significant milestone in my life. It's a moment that some people dread, and some people look forward to. Either way it goes, as long as you keep breathing, you'll reach that same milestone, if you aren't already there. That milestone is the big number 40 that's right this month I turned 40 years old. That is a very significant number because it makes you reflect on life and the experiences that you have had. I heard someone say 40 is when you really step into adulthood. I can honestly say that I have seen a lot and have had the opportunity to meet people from various backgrounds and socio-economic levels.

My upbringing was not that bad. I was raised in a middle-class household. That simply means that we had nice things, but we really didn't have a lot of money. We did get to take some vacations and trips but when I look back, I realize that most of what we did was on a very tight budget. The truth is that this is how a lot of people live. We have the appearance of success or even significance, but we are struggling to maintain an appearance because our lives have become subject to a system that is limited or that places limits on us.

Here's what I've come to know. The middle-class life that many people live in, and some strive for, is really nothing more than a cycle that never ends. Picture this...we get up in the morning and go to work, most of the time to a job that we complain about and work however long they tell us. We come home, tired from working the job we hate, and have no energy to even dream of anything more. For most people, the weekend is the only time they really enjoy life.

For two days (unless we get the most anticipated three-day weekend) we get to dream and feel good about life. Those are the days we feel we have some sort of control. The weekend is the time to dream again. Then we come back to the dreaded Monday. That's the cycle. We do that repeatedly for 25 or 30 years and hope to retire from the cycle so that we can dream and finally get to do what we have always desired to do. I remember being told, all through school, that this was the goal that we were striving for. Once you get out of high school and graduate from college you can get a good job.

I remember, specifically, when we had one of those job fairs at school. They showed us all these options to "spark our interest" in some sort of career path. They would tell us what the job requirements were and then say something like "the average pay for this career is $54,000 to $100,000". As a high school student, those numbers were enticing. I thought for sure if I could land one of those jobs, I would never have anything to worry about. The interesting thing is that I can never once remember being told about entrepreneurship. As a matter of fact, when I told someone about a dream, I had such as being a musician or owning a martial arts school, I was told that those were not "real career paths." So, for most of my life I thought that purpose was attached to a job. I was supposed to do and look like everyone else. In my mind, at the time, destiny was retirement.

Let me share with you how my life changed, and I began the journey to move beyond average and break unproductive cycles to become a high-capacity leader. I remember it was my senior year of High School. In most cases this is the greatest year of your life. This is the year that you have been waiting to get to for 18 years. I really struggled throughout high school, and truth is, unfortunately I got to the point that I didn't really care anymore.

I remember the day like it was yesterday. Me and my buddies were in line to pick up our cap and gowns. We had done all the senior activities, including taking our senior pictures and even participated in "senior skip day". Now we were finally there! It was my turn in line to get my cap and gown. I got to the desk and gave the assistant my name. She looked and said, "your name is not on the list." I couldn't believe it. I knew that there had to be a mistake. She instructs me to talk to the counsellor. I ran into the counsellors' office and told them about the mistake that was made.

The counsellor looked up at me and said, "yeah you're not graduating." That was a devastating moment. I was embarrassed. I was afraid. All I could think was how am I going to go tell all my friends that I had failed? Even worse, how am I going to tell my mother that her oldest son was going to be a high school dropout?

All those hopes and dreams of "making all that money" from the jobs you can get after you graduate and go to college just went down the drain. I thought that my life was over because all I knew was what "they" told me success was. I spent the first several years of my adult life stuck! I worked at one dead end job, after another. I was full of shame, guilt, fear, and discouragement. I understand that there are many people that feel that way. There are many business owners who feel this way. There are many entrepreneurs that feel the same way. You've had people counting on you and it didn't go as planned, and you feel stuck in a cycle.

**The Moment It All Changed.**

It was a Sunday morning. I was sitting in my living room after a long week at my telemarketing job, (that was about the best job I was told that I could get with a GED). I was watching TV and a guy was on a show talking. His name was Dr. Myles Munroe. He began to say some of the most profound statements that I had ever heard. I started paying close attention. He caught my ear because I had never heard anyone describe life the way he did. Then he made a statement that changed everything for me. He said "The tragedy of life is not death. The tragedy of life is a life without purpose."

He said the three most important questions that you can ever answer are these.

1. Who are you?

2. Why are you here?

3. Where are you going?

At that moment I realized that my tragedy wasn't that I wasn't going to a top college to get a degree. The tragedy wasn't that I wasn't working a high paying job. The tragedy wasn't even that I didn't graduate high school. The tragedy was that I didn't know my purpose. So, from that point on I went on a journey to answer those questions and discover why I was on Earth. I discovered that I was here to empower people. To use my gifts and talents to help people discover the best part of themselves. I started teaching martial arts. I started using my gift of music. I got "unstuck". I learned how to "shift from my now, to my next." I realized that failure is not final and that there is always a "next".

That's what this book is all about. It's about you understanding that your life can be massively productive no matter what has happened in your life. You can break that cycle of average and do what no one else in your family has ever done. If a young boy with a GED can go from being in a place of obscurity to now, over a decade later, having touched the lives of tens of thousands of leaders worldwide. I'm totally confident that you can Go Next!

**It may be tough; it may be hard. You may be bruised; you may be scared. But pick up your head, stick out your chest, it's time to flex, because you are about to GO NEXT!**

## Chapter One

# Responds-Ability

*"If you change, everything will change for you. Don't wait for things to change. Change doesn't start out there, change starts within. All change starts with you."*

~ Jim Rohn

For many people, the idea of change sounds good. I believe that most people even desire to see something different in their lives. People hate their jobs and their current financial situation. People are frustrated with not feeling like they're making any type of impact on their society. Frustration comes from having desire, or maybe even a dream, but never seeing that dream come into manifestation.

The easy thing to do is become comfortable in your frustration. Why? Because we simply have no idea how to reach a desired result or how to find our next. In the health and wellness industry that I'm in, I see people who, oftentimes, have a desire to lose weight or gain muscle but never get results. That frustration causes them to become comfortable with the current state of being, so they stop trying altogether. This is the point when the excuses come out. Excuses are the fuel for procrastination. Procrastination is the number one ingredient for "average".

**Whose fault is it anyway?**

Most times, excuses come from us blaming someone else for our lack of results. As a pastor, I see this often when someone feels their life is not going in the direction that they felt it would go. They say, "if you called me more my life would be better." It's always, "it would be better if you did..." The bottom line is that at some point, you must decide that "if it's going to be, it's going to be up to me!" You can't wait on the government to institute the right policies to make your situation better. In my 40 years of living, my socio-economic life has never changed when a particular political party got in office. My pay never went up. NOTHING changed. And you'll hear me say it repeatedly. Nothing will change until you change.

## The Most Hated Word

I believe I have found one of the most hated phrases in the world. That is "personal responsibility." No one likes that word because you can no longer blame the system or "the man". You must look within. That is often painful. It's so much easier to put the blame on someone else. It's so much easier to point the finger. Being a martial artist caused me to learn the principle of personal responsibility.

Going to tournaments, as a martial artist, I always saw this in action. If a competitor lost, he or she would oftentimes find someone to blame. It was the judge's fault. It was the equipment's fault. Humanity has been pushing "blaming" from the beginning of time. Adam blamed Eve. Eve blamed the serpent. No one just said, "it was me! This is my fault, let's correct it."

## The Ability To Respond

The above statement is literally how I define responsibility. It is your ability to respond to your current state of, in a healthy and productive manner. How you respond will determine the level of success you achieve. You can't expect to respond with worry and come out a winner. You can't respond in fear and expect to walk out with faith. You can't respond with doubt and expect to dominate your sphere of influence. It just does not work that way. The 'law of cause and effect' is always in operation. If you bring a certain type of energy to the situation, it will be the cause of a particular outcome.

## You Have The Ability

Our greatest struggle with our current paradigm is that we don't believe in our ability. We rely on someone else's ability to fix our situation. The greatest discovery I've ever made, in my journey of moving from my now, to my next, was when I uncovered my own personal ability. The ability to change my current situation. Here is something that is even more exciting. When you discover your ability no one, nowhere, or no how can ever stop you when you know your ability and begin to respond with courage and optimism. If not, you will go insane doing the same thing, expecting something different to happen. It's time for you to respond to where you are in life, in a way that you've never responded before. This could mean the difference between status quo and significance or just remaining stuck in your current circumstance.

## Freedom And Responsibility

Okay, this may be the most difficult thing to hear but Freedom demands responsibility. Yep, you heard it right. It takes more responsibility to be free than it does to be in bondage. Therefore, most people cannot move into entrepreneurship. It takes too much responsibility and that is just too difficult.

It's easy for you to get up at 5:00am, show up to a job you hate, with people you don't like, holding firmly to the fear of getting fired for one wrong move. You get up because someone is making you. You've shifted the responsibility of your destiny to someone else. You've given them control over your behaviour. But when you have been freed from the "boss man" and you must get up without the thought of someone enforcing it, that's the challenge. You're free from someone else's system. Now you must create your own system. It requires your "ability" to respond, without anyone forcing you.

I do a lot of speaking in prisons and I often hear of someone being released, and in a few months, sometimes weeks, they've returned. It's called recidivism. The recidivism rate is very high in most "correctional" facilities. The reason is because the demand for freedom is too great. You are no longer dependent on someone's ability to invoke your response. You must respond with your own ability. This is what happens when we have momentary breakthroughs in our lives. We start tasting freedom and, at the same time, feel the pain of responsibility. That pain sends us back into the prison of status quo.

It's vital to understand that you were not created to be like everyone else. I like to say that's why no one's fingerprint is the same. We are all created to touch the world in a unique way. Don't become a cheap copy of someone else. Don't just follow the same path of unproductiveness that you've seen.

You were designed to be an original. It is your difference that makes you valuable to the marketplace. It is your difference that causes you to make noise in your sphere of influence. Being the same is the most difficult thing to do in life. When you try to be like everyone else, there's this constant feeling of inadequacy because you don't feel like you'll ever meet the "standard". You always must "fake it until you make it."

Being you is natural. Being you is freedom. Being you is the only way you can truly respond to your environment. When your ability is discovered, you no longer rely on someone else's ability to be a crutch for you.

# Chapter 2

# Believe It Or Not

When I was growing up, there was a show that some of you may remember, called "Ripley's Believe It or Not". The premise of the show was to highlight some unbelievable people or things that seem to be far beyond human comprehension. It was always so fascinating to watch that show because it would stretch your imagination of what was possible. It would display people doing things that seemed humanly impossible but at the same time, it would show how amazing the human will can be. It is shocking when we see people defy the odds of nature. The truth is that these people have just tapped into a part of the mind that has set them free from limitations.

## Hide and Go Seek

Do you recall playing hide and go seek? I do. One person counts, everyone else goes and hides. One, Two, Three...Ready or Not, here I come. Once the person was finished counting, they were on their way. It didn't matter if you were ready or not, they were coming and if you were not prepared and in the right position you would lose the game. This is true also in terms of belief. It could say "believe or not, here I come." In other words, your destiny is true whether you believe or not. The greatness on the inside of you is true whether you believe it or not. Nothing changes simply because you don't believe. The lack of belief causes you to be caught off guard or totally miss opportunities.

In the game, hide and go seek, if you believe that the person is coming, you prepare to be in the right place. In this game, you don't want to be caught, but in life you want to be in the right position so that you can be "tagged". "You're it!" In life, everyone wants to hear those words. It may be that you are looking for a higher paying job; you want to hear "you're it!" Maybe it's some type of gig if you're a musician; you want to hear "you're it!" Maybe it's a major contract of some sort; you want to hear "you're it."

The key is to believe and to position yourself for success because, believe or not, you can have whatever you position yourself for. Let's discuss another way to look at this concept of "hide and go seek". There are some that hide, and there are some that seek. Those who seek, find. Those who hide become subject to those that seek. When you believe in something big enough, you will seek after it until you find it. There is a "no quit" on the inside of you. You'll pursue until you uncover everything that is hiding.

**The Power of Belief**

The ability to believe is one of the most powerful gifts that was given to humanity. Just the fact that you can believe in something before you see it is a miracle within itself. Your life is where it is because that's where you believed it would be. The job you work is a result of your belief. The car you drive is a result of what you believe. You would have never gone to the car lot and applied for the loan, if you did not have some belief on the inside.

True, there are moments where you were surprised you got the loan, but the truth is somewhere on the inside of you, you believed it was possible, that's why you pursued. We never go after our dreams because we "don't" believe it's possible. That's why "many people dream but few people achieve." You will never go beyond your capacity to believe.

## My Black Belt Story

One of my greatest accomplishments was earning my black belt. It was a tough journey full of bumps and bruises, literally. It took hours and hours of training and a ton of dedication. I went through all the ranks one by one and finally that day came. It was the black belt test.

I was about 17 years old, and at the time, you really had to earn that black belt. There was no paying for it or just getting a black belt to make you feel good. The test was all day long. As students, we were tested on everything that we had learned from white belt, all the way up. We were drilled and made to defend various attacks. It was really a test of resilience and determination. The moment came where it was time to fight. I was unbelievably tired. I was exhausted but I still had to fight. We started with five one-on-one fights lasting two minutes each. After this, the testing escalated to two-on-one, three-on-one, all the way up to six-to-one.

The fighting got intense, to say the least. I'll never forget the moment when I threw a kick at Mr. George Baldwin. It was one of the most painful moments of my life. He caught my leg, jumped with me in the air and as I landed on the ground, he landed on my chest. The most excruciating pain shot through my body. I laid on the ground, curled up like a little baby. As I lay there, I was asked the most powerful question. Maybe one of the most important questions that I've ever been asked.

My instructor came over, kneeled, and completely ignored my pain and said, "do you believe you can get up?" In other words, my pain was irrelevant. My current situation was irrelevant. Me being on the ground was irrelevant. What the other guy did to me was irrelevant. The only thing that mattered in that moment was my belief. If I had said, "I can't do it!", I would not have earned my black belt that day and the truth is, I probably wouldn't be a black belt today. I got up hurt, and could barely move, but I finished the fight. It was my greatest moment!!

Here are some very valuable lessons that I learned in that test.

1. When you set out to reach a goal, opposition is set in motion.

2. Tests are not for the purpose of destroying you, they are for the purpose of promoting you.

3. Belief always trumps pain.

4. Belief gives you the strength to keep getting back up!

5. Belief is sometimes greater than skill.

# Chapter 3

# When I Was A Child

I know this is an interesting chapter title. Let me take you down memory lane. Do you remember how it was as a kid? People would ask you what you wanted to be when you grow up. You would say something like, "I want to be a police officer." Some would say "I want to be an astronaut." Some would say things way out there like "I want to live on the moon."

Here's my point, there was no limitation to the imagination. You would think way beyond what anyone even thought was possible. You wanted to be a millionaire, and at that time, you believed you could do anything. Think back with me...what did you want to be when you grew up?

**What Happened?**

Why did you stop dreaming the impossible? As time goes on, we start hearing more and more about what we can't do. As a matter of fact, we probably have heard more of what we can't do, than hearing what we can do. Belief comes by what you hear the most. The result of that is getting caught in cycles of mediocrity. Sad to say that oftentimes the school system does not teach you how to dream. It teaches you how to do the safe thing.

The "safe thing" is to go to school, get good grades to go to college for four more years, get into debt, and then get a job to pay for college debt you've incurred. Now I'm not against school. It's important and kids should always strive to be the best students possible. I'm simply saying that, if we're not careful, we can get trapped in a system that is not designed for us to pursue dreams and goals. If we're not careful, we depend on that system more than what's on the inside of us. It's a cycle. As I said earlier, cycles have an appearance of movement but you're really going in circles.

Let me show you how this works:

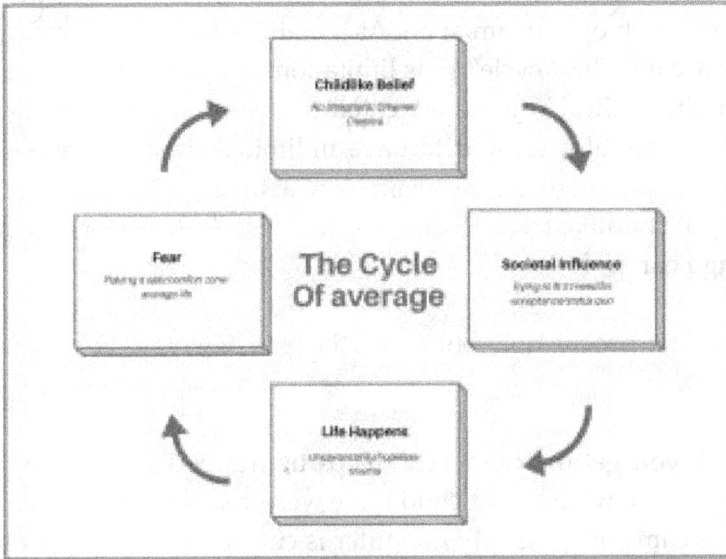

The Cycle Of average

- **Childlike Belief** — No imaginative / Dreams / Creative
- **Societal Influence** — Trying to fit in / Needs for acceptance / status quo
- **Life Happens** — Unexpected injury / Expenses / trauma
- **Fear** — Playing it safe / comfort zone / average life

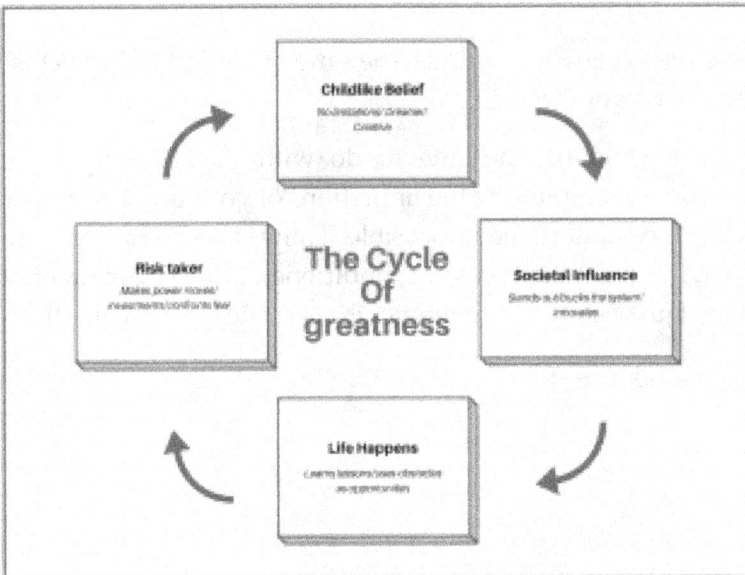

The Cycle Of greatness

- **Childlike Belief** — No limitations / Dreams / Creative
- **Societal Influence** — Stands out / Bucks the system / innovation
- **Life Happens** — Learning lessons / Build character / as opportunities
- **Risk taker** — Makes power moves / investments / comfort is fear

This cycle is what must be broken. The sad truth about it is that we have sold this system as a dream. What has been called the "American Dream", for many people, is not much of a dream at all. As a matter of fact, it has caused them to forfeit their dream. This "cycle" puts limitations on your life. You were created to have a limitless life. You were created to dream and dream big. Not only that, but you were also created to have unlimited dreams. Once one dream comes to pass, you can dream again. I'm a firm believer that it's vital to rediscover that childlike faith. Rediscover that child's dream and go for it!

**Overcoming Fear**

Fear is the fuel for procrastination. Fear is the seed of worry. Fear causes dreams to lie dormant.

Okay, I think you get the point fear keeps us trapped in the same mundane cycles that get us nowhere. As a child there were very few things that we feared in terms of dreams or goals. My daughter is currently three years old and has no fear when it comes to accomplishing something that she feels strongly about. If she wants to climb on the couch and jump, she just does it. If she believes that she can do it, even if it's with my help, she's going for it.

Sometimes it's risky, and a few times she's hurt herself, but her belief is always greater than the risk or the pain.

Thinking like a child has nothing to do with your maturity level. It has everything to do with removing the limitations of your mind and dreaming big. It has to do with dreaming the impossible. Things that most think are silly you pursue. When I was a child, I was not conditioned by a system that told me how far I could go. I just believed, somehow, that I could do amazing things.

**Here is an exercise.**

1. Write down all your biggest dreams and goals. Don't put any limitations on yourself. Dream things that seem ridiculous. The idea is to expand your mind and dream BIG again.

2. Do something that you have never done before. For some that may be climbing a mountain. For others, that may be reciting a speech in front of a crowd which, for a lot of people, is bigger than climbing a mountain. The point is to challenge yourself.

3. Get some exposure. You will never go beyond what you've been exposed to. Go to a seminar. Go view houses that you can't afford, "Yet." Once your mind is expanded it can never go back to the way it was.

# Chapter 4

# Reset

B eing able to "reset" is one of the most powerful operations that has ever existed. The reason I say that is because it is a function that allows me to go back and start all over again. It doesn't matter where you are in the process, once you reset, you have a new opportunity to do something different or to see something that you may have missed. It gives you another chance. The truth is, this is how it is when pursuing dreams and breaking cycles. We always have a chance to "reset."

If you are between the ages of about 30 and 40 years old, you probably remember one of the greatest gaming systems ever made…. Nintendo. Yep, that's right! Super Mario Brothers, Tecmo Bowl, Double Dribble, The Legend of Zelda, Kung Fu fighter and one of my favorites Mike Tyson's Punch out. These games are classic.

They all had various levels; each having differing degrees of challenges. The problem that I often experienced was that in the middle of trying to get to the next level the game would freeze up. It would get stuck on that screen. No matter what I did, nothing happened. The music was still playing and sometimes the characters around me were still moving but I was stuck. The game was set. I couldn't go any further and it was frustrating especially when I thought that I was finally about to conquer that level and move on to the next.

That is life. That's what happens to so many people. Right when you get to the brink of a breakthrough in your life, you get stuck. Everything is moving around you, but you can't go anywhere. Bills are still moving. Life is still moving all around you, but it seems like you can't go anywhere. The unfortunate thing about this scenario is that it often starts early in life. Your mind is stuck on a particular 'picture' and you can't get past that. If you've only seen one thing all your life, you can never get to the next level.

## The Mind-Set

Mindset is an image that sets your desire and expectation. Sometimes a game would only go to a certain level and every time it got to that level, it would get stuck. There was some type of glitch in the system that caused it to only go to that one level. This leads me to believe that there is a glitch in our thinking that only allows us to go so far.

That glitch must be corrected for us to go to the next level of life. In that gaming system, the "reset" button was right there in the front. Anytime I got stuck, the only thing I could do was reset. The good thing about Nintendo is that they had cheat codes. I could reset and start all over again where I left off. In a similar manner, our lives must be constantly reset. Sometimes there are certain images that get stuck in our minds that we must get rid of so that we can move on. Sometimes this is hard because you can be so close to your dream, but it's necessary. That's what failure really is. It's an opportunity to reset. When you lose your job, it is an opportunity to reset. When a relationship fails, it's an opportunity to reset. Whatever you do, don't get stuck on that screen!

## Cheat Codes

I mentioned earlier that Nintendo had what were called "cheat codes". The thing I really liked about cheat codes was that you could start in a better place than you left off. On "Mike Tyson's Punch Out" I could punch in the right code and start in a place that would get me straight to Mike Tyson. What I'm saying is when you change your mind you change the set-point. You don't always have to keep going back to the same place. You can start in a place that you've never been.

There are some cheat codes for life, believe it or not. You can learn from someone else's experiences. You can do personal development. You can get into a new environment around people that want to succeed. See, you can skip levels. Just because someone had to experience certain things doesn't mean you have to. I'm not saying that success is easy, or you can cheat your way to success. Please don't misunderstand. The principle is that if you work from the right paradigm, you will do what others could only dream of.

You must set your mind on greater things. You must enhance your vision. If I'm going to see something different, it is vital for me to "Reset" my mind.

Here is a question that you must ask yourself.

Where is my current paradigm? What has my life been like? What is it that has me stuck? Once you discover that, it's time to "Reset."

One of the ways I reset my mind is to drive and look at houses that "I can't afford, at this time." I talk to people that have reached the level I seek to attain. I fix my mind on something greater than where I am so that I won't get stuck in the same place that I've always been.

**Problem or Promise?**

A major issue as to why we never "reset" our mind, is that we focus on the problem. We look at our current issues and the challenges of our lives. That becomes the focus. You cannot focus on the negatives of your life. Film starts out negative, in the dark, until the light shines on
it. Light represents new information. Once that light shines, the thing that was negative becomes a beautiful picture. Light is necessary for focus. My point is that new information will cause you to refocus your mind. It will give you a new picture of what's possible.

Here are some questions to help you evaluate your current paradigm.

- What is the last thing you watched on T.V?
- Who is in your inner circle?
- What are you posting?

## What is the last thing you watched on T.V?

Let me tell you why this is so important. You will always look for, and gravitate to, what you are subconsciously or even consciously aware of. When I say subconsciously or consciously, I'm ultimately talking about your paradigm. If you are rushing home to watch the latest drama filled reality T.V. show, you are defining the paradigm that you live in. If you wake up in the morning and the first thing you do is turn on the news, which is mostly negative, you have defined your paradigm. I decided to cancel my cable, so that I can redefine my paradigm. I like to say that Television does exactly what it says, it "tells-you-a vision."

## Who Is In Your Inner Circle?

It is said that you are a sum of the five people that you hang around the most. If that is true, if you are constantly around five broke people, you'll be number six. Have you ever noticed that football players are generally around other football players? Basketball players are generally around other basketball players. People who like to hunt generally hang with other hunters. Here is the point: check who you hang around and evaluate your current paradigm. Are these people helping you get results or are they feeding into your mediocre life? I know that's tough. Some of those people you've been around since second grade. But the question is are you ready to graduate from the second grade?

## What Are You Posting?

I know many of you say "well, Social Media is just that...Social Media. It's not real." I've heard that so many times. Let's slow down and consider the reality of this. One of the popular platforms asks a question, "What's On Your Mind?" On your status the objective is to tell the world what your thoughts are. Basically, you are telling the world what your current paradigm looks like. Maybe it should say "What is your paradigm?"

Every post that you make is a confession of where you are in your mind-set. Go through your timeline and evaluate what you've said over the last year. Are those statements progressive and productive or are those statements revealing your self-limiting beliefs? Are they revealing your lack of focus? Are they revealing your lack of discipline? These are very important things to consider. Some of the social platforms will actually do a "throwback" for you. They will show you what you said a month ago, a year ago or even further back than that. Evaluate if that way of thinking is the reason that there are no results in your life?

To get to the next level, you must determine where you are. When you discover where you are, you must find the map to where you're going. When you find the map, it's simple, just
GO!!

## It's Time To Reset!

## Chapter 5

# In The Middle

*Every threat to the status quo is an opportunity in disguise.* ~
Jay Samit

In "the middle" is the place where most people live their lives. It's a safe place. It's the comfort zone. The middle is neither good nor bad. It does not offend anyone or challenge anything.

When a person doesn't want to stir up any type of conflict they say, "I'm neutral on this one." Neutral requires nothing extra from you. Think about it. Have you ever put your car in neutral? Your car becomes subject to the environment. Depending on where you're parked, you will either go forward or backward and, at some point, you will stop or crash. In "neutral" someone else can come and pull you in whatever direction they want you to go.

If you remain neutral, you remain subject to whatever happens. A life in neutral depends on the economy to succeed. If the economy is down, then your life is down. If the economy is up, your life is up. That is not the way to live. We were not designed to live life in the middle. We are designed to live on the top. We are designed to live without limits.

## Middle Class

I recently took a personal poll of people that I know and realized something very interesting. Most people, in terms of finances, make a living in a place called "middle class". As a matter of fact, most of what we're taught in school teaches how to live in most effectively "the middle".

**Let's do a little fact check concerning the "middle class"**

Middle Class income ranges from $25,000 - $80,000 and some say up to $150,000.

According to the Washington post the median household income is $56,500.

The average middle-class American is $130,000 in debt according to Time. (Over $15,000 being credit card debt)

Income grew 26% over the last few years.

But wait before you get too excited.

Food costs also grew by 37% and medical costs by 57%. The cost of living has exceeded the average income. Which means people are making more but they are also paying more. (AOL Finance)

Forty seven percent of middle-class workers would not have $400 in case of an emergency.

The worst one yet. The average retirement income is $1,298.98 a month. So, wait, I work 30-40 years (according to money.usnews) for a company and after I've given most of my life, you give me a plaque and $1,298.88 a month.

Let me tell you why all that was so important to note. If we are conditioned to live in the middle that means that we are conditioned to never get ahead. This isn't just about money, it's about THE NEXT. Living life in the middle is guaranteeing one thing, a cycle of frustration. Get out of the middle. It will require challenging what you've been taught. Sometimes it will cause you to lose friends that you've grown up with. But you must make up your mind. The middle is not the place for you. You're not designed to just be in the middle.

## Stand Alone

When you decide that you are ready to move out from the average, or "normal", it often requires that you stand alone. Most people will never understand why you would try to do something different. A lot of people really care about you and want the best for you. However, here is where you must be careful. People will give you advice based on their limited paradigm. If you want to step out and start a business, it's not a good idea to get advice from someone who only desires to work for someone else. Their paradigm is only going to be from the place of employment. They can't "see" entrepreneurship.

It's always funny to me when someone tells me what I'm doing won't work and they've never tried it. There is safety in wise counsel, but wise counsel simply means to receive counsel that has been where you're going or is in the same paradigm of your vision. You can't receive wise counsel from someone that is not thinking on the level that you're going. As a martial artist, it would be insane for me to get coached by someone that has never fought a day in their life. How can they tell me when to kick and they have never thrown a kick?

Therefore, sometimes it requires that you go by yourself on this journey. Results always require that you stand out, stand alone and just go. Along the way, there will be people that you will connect with that can help you get to the next phase of your journey. Standing alone does not mean doing it alone. You will always have people around you who are no longer "middle of the road" people, that will help stretch you and expose you to greater possibilities.

Let me dig deeper into this concept of "living "in the middle." Another definition of "living in the middle", is simply being the same as the "majority", neither hot nor cold. It's lukewarm. You just kind of blend in with everyone else. The sad thing is that society is really set up for you to live in the middle. Most programs and even education teaches you how to maintain your life in the middle.

So, the question is how do we get out of the middle? The first thing is that you must decide. You must decide that there is a better way for you to live. I once heard someone say, a decision is "to achieve a specific result with no possibility of retreat". I love that definition for several reasons.

The phrase "specific result" always catches my attention when I quote that definition. A "specific result" speaks to a goal. It is a well-crafted, well-thought out, goal that you desire to achieve. It often is discovered by an unshakeable passion. Bill Hybels called it "Holy Discontent." There must be something that you desire to have that you will do whatever it takes to achieve. No matter how long it takes. No matter how tough it becomes. No matter how crazy people think you are, you will not quit. WHY? Because you want RESULTS.

## No Retreat No Surrender

There are some people that want to get out of the middle however there is one thing that's stopping them, the deadly habit of quitting. Starting is the easy part, it's finishing that becomes the greatest challenge. I've seen so many people walk into my wellness office and say, "I'm ready to get rid of this weight." They will cry. They will thank me for giving them a plan. They will spend money over the course of a few weeks, and I will never hear from them again.

## What Happened?

They had emotional desire but not dedicated desire. Emotional desire is when you move on a feeling without counting the cost. Dedicated desire does not care what the
cost is.

If you want results you must have the mindset; No Retreat No Surrender!!

# Chapter 6

# In The Process Of Time

T here is a saying in my favorite book, "The Bible", that says "every purpose is beautiful in its time" (Ecclesiastes 3:11). I love that because it lets us know that if you learn how to maximize time you will eventually see your dreams and visions come true.

Everything has a process of time. Time is very interesting. Time is the currency of life. Anything you give your time to, you're really giving your life to. In other words, life costs time. You pay for life with time. When you run out of time you have run out of life. You can't get it back once it's gone.

Here is another unique element of time. It never stops. I remember taking those dreaded timed tests. I wasn't very focused in school, so I would get distracted and sometimes just start staring into space. The problem is that even though I stopped, time kept going. The fact that I didn't finish was irrelevant. When the time finished, the teacher would always say "close your books and put your pencil down". They would also remind us that we couldn't go back to correct any answers or to answer questions we did not finish.

**The Test is Timed**

This is an important lesson about life. In essence, you are in a timed test. That's life. When the test is over you can't go back and finish what you didn't complete. The book is closed. That means that you must use the time you have been given to complete the assignment you have on the Earth.

Luck is not what makes people get results. Success does not come to those that come from the best neighborhoods or go to the best schools. It comes to those that learn how to maximize time. It is to those that use time to do the necessary things that guarantee the desired results. Consider this, a person may have more money to spend but when it comes to time, everyone is on an equal playing field.

*Everyone gets a daily allowance of 24 hours.*

The difference between greatness and average is how those 24 hours are spent. In other words, how are you investing your time? People often say they don't have enough time to do certain things or to pursue dreams. I often want to ask them, "how did you get less time than everyone else?" It's not about having enough time, it's about what you choose to do with that time that you have. People who get results understand this and they invest their time wisely.

Most people spend so much time on things that don't matter. We spend time worrying about things we can't change or on things that will never happen. We spend time in front of a television for hours watching people who are living their dream, while hating the jobs we work. It's okay to admire people's dreams but it's not okay to invest your time watching them and neglect your own dream. So many people spend hours talking about the superstar athlete or entertainer. The question is when are you going to start investing your time and conversation on your own goals?

Remember, life is like vapor. You are here today and gone tomorrow. You are given an entry date and an exit. Your time begins when you are conceived and ends when you take your last breath. So, what you do in between those times is vital. For some children, around 12 years old is when they really start making decisions that can affect their lives going forward. That's usually when you develop habits, some good and some not so good. That's when a child's life begins to be influenced by more than just your parents.

A lot of times, the most difficult part of our life, in terms of pursuing success, is to deprogram our minds. In those formative years, we were subject to certain ways of thinking that created self-limiting beliefs. Those self-limiting beliefs are what cause us to invest our time into things that are unproductive. We don't think certain levels of success belong to us and if we pursue those things, we are "wasting our time." I've heard it so many times, "Stop wasting your time and get a regular job." You're called crazy and, sometimes even irresponsible for not being like everyone else. The system that we live in has us spending 8 to 16 hours of our day at a place that you dread, take a few dollars for those hours and be satisfied with those results. People pay you just enough to make you comfortable not dreaming.

Most of your day is given to someone else's dream, so we must begin to look at jobs differently. Although necessary, because someone must work, I don't believe our jobs should be viewed as lifelong activities, rather opportunities to learn skills that will assist us in getting to our next place in life. In other words, while you work, maximize that time. It's not about what you're making, it's about what you're learning.

I worked for the first part of my adult life as a telephone account executive. Okay, that's a politically correct way of saying "telemarketer." I hated those jobs. I had to call people, and interrupt their day, trying to get them to change their long-distance service or get them to get some type of insurance. I've done cold calling. I've managed customer office supply accounts. I've done just about anything that you can name in phone sales.

Call Center jobs can be very stressful. Most people can't last because you're constantly being cursed out or called out of your name. One day it dawned on me, while I was making calls. I was dealing with an irate customer, and I had to de-escalate the call. Once the call ended, I realized what a success it was, and how I was learning the skill of communication. I was learning how to present ideas to people from a different perspective. I was learning how to cast vision. I was learning how to communicate with people that didn't have the same ideas as me. I was learning the art of persuasion.

That was a turning point for me. I used the time that I was on the phone, as training because I knew that I had a greater call on my life. My dream was bigger than the call center, but it was a great training ground. That's the power of working a job, even if it's only for a season. You get to learn skills that you can't even learn in school. If you work a job, begin to focus on what you're learning. That job may not be your career path, however when you "maximize the time", you can learn valuable skills that can be essential in the fulfillment of your purpose. I appreciate my time in call centers because it has helped me communicate to thousands of people on stages.

**Budget Your Time**

Just like money, you must budget your time. If you want to know where it's going and how much you're "spending". Most people never think in terms of budgeting your time but if it's something that can be spent, it's something that can be budgeted. It's important to know how your time is being spent and how productive you are with that time. What is your ROI (Return on Investment)?

If you spend four hours watching the latest sitcoms, what is your return on investment? If you are on social media for five hours, what is your return on investment?

So, again, it's very important to be intentional about where you invest your time. If you've ever said, "I lost track of time", you've just admitted that you are not intentionally budgeting your time. That statement is usually the excuse for not getting a desired result.

If you protect your time, you can predict your future.

# Chapter 7

# Fearless

❧

Fear is the greatest enemy of greatness. Fear causes you to procrastinate and never pursue a better future. Fear is what causes you to forfeit destiny.

Truth is, anytime you set out to that you've never seen done before, there is an internal conversation with fear. Fear rises and says, "you can't do that!" Fear starts telling you you're not good enough. You must talk back to fear. I mean that literally. You must tell fear that you believe in yourself and your potential. Fear comes, but you don't have to live fearfully. Living fearfully is dangerous. That's a lifestyle of fear.

## Do It Afraid

I recall, in my fight days, that every time I would go into the ring, there would be this extreme fear that would come over me. At times, I would feel like I couldn't move. In those moments, I could have let fear win. I could have set back and said, "there is no way I can go out there". But instead, I would go out afraid and, without fail, once the first punch or kick was thrown, the fear went away, and I was able to function with ease. I've seen people fight the whole fight in fear, which usually doesn't go very well. But, in most cases, once you start you no longer have time to get distracted by the voice of fear.

Therefore, I say, "do it afraid!" Just go! Once you get started you will outrun fear. Fear doesn't have a chance to stop you.

To move deeper into purpose, you must starve fear. Let me explain what I mean. A lot of times we take advice from the wrong people. I always hear Grant Cardone say, "stop taking advice from quitters." I think this is so important. People often give you advice out of their own place of failure. Something didn't work for them, so they quit trying and tell you it won't work for you. They tell you how broke they were and how horrible their experience was. They are feeding your fears.

In the "Google age" that we are in, it's so easy to pull up articles that feed your fear. You can find hundreds of doubters and non-believers. If you're in network marketing, you can find all types of articles saying that network marketing is a scam. If you are opening a restaurant, you can research the reasons why the food service you're offering won't work in your region. The media will tell you that the economy is too bad for you to make anything happen. You must choose wisely in what you hear. Faith comes by hearing and so does fear.

## What Are You Afraid Of?

This is a critical question. It's hard to conquer something when you haven't identified what it is. If you don't know what you're afraid of you will never step out and accomplish the things that you desire. Identify your fear and then identify the root of your fear. In other words, once you know what you're afraid of, then you will need to find out why. If you are afraid to start a business, what is the root of that fear? Maybe it's because you've only listened to the statistics about how many businesses fail. Maybe your parents started a business that didn't seem to work.

Fear can be rooted in a variety of things, which include the fear of failure and the fear of death. Think about it. People say they are afraid of flying in airplanes. That's not true, they are afraid of dying. People say they're afraid of spiders. Not necessarily, you are afraid of what a spider could do to you.

If you take the dying equation out, in most cases, the fear goes with it. Same thing in pursuing your dreams. It's not the fear of starting a business, non-profit, ministry outreach, or applying for a promotion. It's the fear that it might not work, or you might not be good enough for it. It's the fear of failure. If you take the failure element out, then the fear goes away.

If there was no way that you could fail, what would you do? This is a very good way to discover your purpose in life. If all obstacles were removed, and fear never showed its face, I guarantee that your life would be totally different than it is now. That tells me that it is going to be imperative that you learn how to overcome fears and learn how to walk out your destiny.

So, the ultimate question is, "how do you become fearless?" Let's go back to the concept of what you're hearing. We must start there. In the morning you must pour into your mind something that brings you into a mindset of victory. If you have not heard of the term "personal development", you may want to familiarize yourself with it. Start by listening to something motivational, something that feeds your confidence and starves your fears. Listen to Les Brown tell you that "there is greatness on the inside of you" or Tony Robbins tell you "How you can reach your goals" or Grant Cardone shows how you can "make money, keep money, and multiply money".

Listen to stories of people that have overcome. Read about people that have succeeded. Get away from people that always doubt and talk about how they failed. Stop taking advice from other fearful people. I have the privilege of traveling around the world and speaking to audiences about leadership, purpose, and helping individuals discover their worth and value. I recall a time when I was preparing to fly to Tanzania, East Africa and just days before, a plane had crashed on the same path my flight would take. The news played that story over and over and over.

I made the mistake of watching it every time it played, until it came to a point that I started questioning if I should go on the trip. Someone even called me and said, "are you sure you should take this trip, with all these planes falling out of the air?" As I said before, faith and fear both come by hearing. I had to change what I was hearing. I had to start talking to people that travelled frequently and were not afraid. I had to turn the news off, so I wouldn't hear that story repeatedly. I had to focus on my assignment. I had to starve the fear. If I had not made that flight, I probably would've never taken an international trip, as that experience opened the door for so many other trips and opportunities.

Like worry, generally what you are afraid of, will never happen. You can't allow yourself to be afraid of a possibility. You must learn how to reverse the fear of negative possibilities and have faith in the positive ones. The difference is that the negative will cause you to never move.

The positive will cause you to go after what you believe.

**What Does A Fearless Life Look Like?**

A fearless life is a life that will take the risk. Living fearlessly means that you will do what others want to do. You don't see obstacles, you see opportunities. Spending time in Kilimanjaro helped me see this clearly. I always started my trip at the Key's Hotel, which is a major tourist spot for people coming to climb the mountain. I've seen so many people come all that way, spend their money, and only get to the foot of the mountain. For them, fear stepped in, and they turned around. But for the fearless, they saw this as an opportunity of a lifetime that they could not pass up.

I've heard it said that you must take advantage of every "opportunity of a lifetime" within the lifetime of the opportunity. You just don't get a second chance, in some things. Don't let fear cause you to watch someone else do what you know you had in you to do.

Zig Ziglar defined fear as "False Evidence Appearing Real". Here is a neat scientific fact...darkness is not real. In other words, you can't measure darkness. You can't turn on darkness. There is no speed of darkness. Darkness is simply the absence of light. So, if you want it to get darker, there is no switch that says turn up the darkness. You must take the light out. Fear and darkness are about the same. Most of what we are afraid of, in terms of pursuit of destiny, is not even real; it's just that something is missing. The thing that is missing is called courage.

Fear is simply the absence of courage. Courageous people always experience the greatest moments in life. Fearful people are employed by the courageous. Fearful people pay hundreds of dollars to go watch the courageous live out their destiny. Fearful people never get results. Courageous people don't stop until they see results. It's time that you live a courageous life.

Courage is not always the absence of fear itself, it is facing fear head on and overcoming it. Courage is knowing the risk but deciding the reward is greater. Courageous people are willing to put it all on the line. If it takes your life, your attitude is, "at least I gave it all." Courageous people are the ones that we read about in history books. The ones that fell and got back up, no matter how hard they fell. What category are you going to live in? Are you going to be the one that never saw results because of some false reality?

Turn up the courage. It's time to see what you really have on the inside. It's time for you to unlock the fullness of your potential and walk out the life you were designed to live. See, when you turn on the light, darkness flees and what's visible are endless possibilities you didn't know existed. When you "turn on" the courage, you see things that you never knew you could be capable of. You overcome things that you thought would have you trapped forever. You tap into hidden resources and hidden talents when you turn up the courage. You become bold in expressing who you are and why you are.

Courage is the key to living a fearless life.

# Chapter 8

# Living On The Edge

Most people in the world are looking for a place called comfort. I hear it all the time, "I just want to be comfortable." The "comfortable" place is easy, and it doesn't take much effort. It can also be called a "safe place." Some people even call it "contentment" or stability.

The systems that are set up in this world are designed to show you how to live the most comfortable life possible. Let me be clear, there is absolutely nothing wrong with living safe. There is nothing wrong with being comfortable. But you must remember comfortable people have very little impact on their generation. Comfortability is fuel for average.

Greatness is only developed in an environment of risk. There comes a point in your life that you must live dangerously, if you want something big to happen in your life. I know you say, "what if I do that and something goes wrong?" The reality is something probably will go wrong. Something will happen. You will have some obstacles. But people that take risks, prepare for things that will go wrong and make the adjustments.

**The Mindset**

The devastating thing about comfortability is that it is more than just about settling for where you are. Comfortability is a mindset. It is a routine, in the thought process, that causes you to become blinded to other possibilities or anything that breaks your routine. Routine is not all bad, if it is a routine that keeps you uncomfortable and causes growth. For example, if you are in the gym and you only do enough exercise to be comfortable, you're not going [to see results. It just won't happen. You must look for what is going to make you hurt or stretch you. You must look for what makes you feel uncomfortable. It's called "pain with a purpose."

## Pain with a Purpose

Safe people never go to the gym because they are afraid of that pain. When you see someone with health results, you can be assured that they have gone through the pain that most are not willing to endure.

Life should be an adventure. It should be exciting. If your life is all about clock-in/clock-out, go to bed, get up and do it all over again the next day, you must question if you've even started living. Many people "die" in their career and get buried after they retire. That's not how you were designed to live. You were designed to live out loud. Your very "make up" (who you were created to be) is adventurous. It's time to start living out your potential. If all you do is wake up, to go to work, there's a great possibility you're living out someone else's dream. If you're going to work 12 hours a day, you might as well do it for your own dream.

This is what I call "living on the edge". Living on the edge will always be an enemy of reason. Reason justifies complacency. Reason gives you excuses as to why you can't. Living on the edge is that process of ignoring reason. When you live on the edge, other people look at you and call you crazy. They advise you based on their personal fear of what you're doing. I can hear them now, "You better not do that."

"You might get hurt" or "you know what happened to the last person that tried that." I have learned that if everyone else is not doing something that's probably what I should be doing. That may not be true in all cases, but it is in most.

## Just Jump

I remember when I was a teenager, maybe 18 or so, and a local car lot held a promotion to get people to come back to check out their cars. They had a huge platform with a sign that read, "free bungee jumping". Me and a few of my friends thought it would be cool to go and check this whole event out. We watched person after person climb to the top and then climb right back down. The risk was too great for anyone to jump, well at least in their eyes.

One of my buddies had this crazy idea that maybe we should be the ones that make that jump. I wasn't too sure about that, but it was something I had never done before and it seemed easy enough, right? I climbed up this crane, or something like that. When I got up there, something happened. I came face to face with fear, and in my mind, I was telling myself "You better walk back down like everyone else." I've always been a person that really didn't want to do what everyone else did, although, admittedly I did more often than I wanted to. I looked down and said, "I can't do this." But I knew that I would be like others that didn't jump.

While I was up there, I heard something that, for some reason, has stuck with me, even until this day. Someone yelled, JUST JUMP, YOU'RE HOLDING UP THE LINE! Now I understand what that meant. They were saying, because you are procrastinating you are holding up progress. I wanted to turn around, because being that high in the air was, well you guessed it, uncomfortable. But when I heard that voice say, "just jump", I was faced with another feeling.

**This Time It Was Different.**

It was a belief. It was confidence. It was faith. So, I jumped. As I was going down, I thought, "I did it!" No one else jumped, and the crazy part was that after I jumped, everyone else jumped when their turn came. It was one of the greatest experiences I ever had in my life! It was uncomfortable. It was crazy. It was dangerous (although there was an airbag in case something went wrong). In your life there are times when you must jump. Think of how much you miss when you don't jump? Life is too short to be comfortable.

Now this is going to sound like a contradiction or a paradox, but you must be comfortable with being uncomfortable. My point is, if you want to grow, get used to living edgy.
That's the only way that you will see anything happen in your life, outside of the mundane, status quo existence. The world was changed by people that lived on the edge and jumped.

**Here are just a few of those names:**

- ○ Wilbur and Orville Wright
- ○ Henry Ford
- ○ Martin Luther King Jr
- ○ Steve Jobs
- ○ Mark Zuckerberg
- ○ Rosa Parks
- ○ Bill Gates
- ○ Mark Hughes

Those are just a few names. Just think if you decide to live outside of your comfort zone, you may be the one that shifts the direction of the culture. You may be the one that changes life as we know it, but for sure you will change how your family lives. You will do more than just exist; you will create a legacy. The reason you must get unstuck, and break unproductive cycles, is because you must leave a legacy that the next generation can build on.

**Leave a Legacy of Innovation**

Most of what is passed on to our kids is the same system of mundane, status quo living. We teach our kids how to be average because we lived average lives. When you live on the edge, it teaches your kids that anything is possible. It teaches them not to fear being different. It gives them the benefit and power of not "fitting in". They will know that they don't have to do what everyone else is doing, or dress like everyone else or listen to the songs that everyone else is listening to. They will become natural innovators or creators.

People who think life starts and stops with them, will only play it safe because they can't see past their current world. Here is what I call a selfish life, which is like what I've shared in previous chapters. A person works 40 hours a week, at a job they hate, just to barely pay the bills with hopes of someday retiring with a retirement package that's just enough to make it; and most of the time, having to get another job to work the rest of their life. That's not legacy, that's what you get when you never live on the edge or take risks. It seems like it's better when you "stay safe" but in the long run, it's the worst thing that you can do for your family.

**Never Take Another Vacation**

Yep, that's right! You should desire to never take another vacation in your life. The only reason people plan vacation is because they want to get away from their life. Every vacation I went on had two different dynamics. I was so excited that I got a week or two to get away from the life I hated. Then, I was almost depressed thinking about the fact that I had to go back to the life I hated. It was a temporary fix that often put me more into debt.

When you take the limits off your life, you don't need vacations to get away. You just live. Your life is an amazing adventure of meeting new people and seeing new places. I've been all over the world. When I leave one country, I get excited because I know I'm about to prepare for the next adventure. While I'm in one country doing leadership seminars, I'm looking forward to the next place. I get to see places that I never thought I would see. I'm not lucky and I don't have some type of special "thing" on me. I just took the risk one day and went to Africa with a group of people that I barely knew. That one leap of faith. That "edgy" decision opened the world to me.

Get out the box. Live your life on the edge. Go do something that you have never done before. Find something that you are terrified of and face it. Do it. Starve that fear.

Don't do this just for you. Do this for those that are following you.

JUST JUMP!!!!!!!!

# Chapter 9

# Not Guilty

A s I began to study successful and unsuccessful people, including high-capacity leaders, I began to recognize the things that separate the two that we, oftentimes, don't know is a major barrier to progress. That is, guilt. Most times, when we hear the word guilt, we think of someone doing something wrong and the feeling afterwards. That is a part of it; however, the other element is the feeling of guilt because of success. They feel guilty because they are achieving results, in certain areas of their life, while others close to them, are not.

For some of us, who were taught things such as "having money is for evil people," when we get money, we feel like we've done something wrong. You may start a business but become afraid of succeeding because you know you're going to have to leave some people behind. Success always demands new environments. Success demands change.

The feeling of guilt comes when you look at the people or places you must leave; and feel bad or like you shouldn't do it. Those people will play on that feeling by saying something like, "So you're just going to leave us at this job?" "You think you're something now that you live in that neighborhood." These are the types of things that average people say to those that decide to be "above average". The statement, "misery loves company" is true. People want you to stay where they are and when you change, it makes them uncomfortable.

In Grant Cardone's book, "Be Obsessed or Be Average", he states that "people will always criticize you in areas that they have failed in." I think this is so important to note because if you allow people to tell you what you can or cannot do, you will never do anything. I have people tell me, all the time, "you shouldn't be in business because you're a preacher." You shouldn't write "self-help" books because it's not godly but most of those people are living unhappy lives.

My point is, don't let anyone make you feel guilty for pursuing your passion or dreams. If you must leave some people behind, that's okay. My wife always says to me, "the best way to prove your point is to get results."

When people talk, don't feel guilty, get RESULTS.

**You Have Permission.**

You must give yourself permission to succeed. Sometimes we disqualify ourselves from success. It's not what other people say, it's what we say to ourselves. You must tell yourself that you will succeed. It's called "self-talk". When you talk negatively to yourself, you are telling yourself that you don't have permission to succeed.

I always tell people that "whatever follows your "I am", will become your reality." If you say, "I am broke!", "I'm weak!" "I'm never going to be better than this!". Those things become the realities of your life. You have disqualified yourself from ever winning in life.

**Don't Forfeit**

Every athlete has heard the word forfeit. It's when an opponent thinks there is no way they can win, so they just decide to not "show up". They give up because they feel outnumbered and weaker than their opponent. They don't even take the chance at victory. I remember being told, in one fight, that I didn't have a chance. I was told to just forfeit, so I wouldn't get hurt because the guy was way bigger than me. Well, there was no way I was giving up.

I was more determined than ever to prove them wrong. I went out there and fought hard and ended up winning. Why? I gave myself permission to win. What have you forfeited because you thought there was no way you could succeed? Release yourself into the best days of your life. Don't wait on someone else to tell you to go for it. Don't wait for someone else to tell you that you're good enough or strong enough or smart enough. Here's a reality check. People may never tell you any of those things.

You will be waiting forever, if you think that people are going to give you permission to be great. People will give you permission to be average. People will give you permission to be normal. They will celebrate when you get a new job. They will even celebrate you when you get a degree. They will encourage you to be like them. But as soon as you say I'm quitting my job or I decided not to go to school, so that I can go into a business for myself, the same people will call you crazy.

## What's The Problem?

If your life hasn't progressed from one year to the next, you must know that there is a problem. I'll tell you the problem. The problem is you're telling yourself "No". Every opportunity that comes your way you say, "No". Every door that opens you say, "No".

## Just Say YES!

In 1987, First Lady of the United States of America, Nancy Reagan came up with a campaign that became very popular. It was, "Just Say No." It had a positive message, with a negative phrase. "No" is a negative. It was good for telling youth to stay away from drugs and alcohol. In those terms, it was a powerful message.

Here is the problem, according to medmd.com, toddlers hear the word "no" 400 times a day. So everyday you're told what you can't do and never told what you can do. Most of what we've heard all our life is things like "You're not tall enough." You're not old enough." "You don't know enough."

## I Hear Voices

The voice in your head is, oftentimes, the voice that you heard in the formative years of your life. Much of what you say is based on the foundation of the voice that you've heard the most. If you've heard "no" 400 hundred times a day, for much of your life, you are probably going to say "no" to almost everything. Are there times when saying "no" is necessary? Absolutely. But we often get stuck in cycles of average because we say "no" to everything.

Saying "yes" is giving yourself permission to succeed. It's you saying to yourself, "let's go for it!" You may not understand it all but just because you said "yes" you are giving your potential the opportunity to reveal itself. You have no way of knowing what you can do until you say "yes" to trying something that you've never done. I've found myself in some amazing places, and in the presence of some amazing people, simply because I said "yes".

Success is not running from you. It's looking for you. It's trying to find you because you are a success magnet. Give yourself permission to receive the success that's chasing you down.

As we end this chapter, I want to also give you permission to forgive yourself. Yes, forgive yourself. This is key to freedom and gets you on the move to amazing results. You made some mistakes in life and that's okay. Everyone has made mistakes, some greater than others, but you must make the decision to put them behind you and move forward. That's what counts!

**Here are some affirmations you can say:**

- I give myself permission to succeed.

- I give myself permission to be great.

- I give myself permission to win no matter what.

- I give myself permission to be an influencer.

- I give myself permission to be wealthy.

- I give myself permission to live my best life.

- I give myself permission to leave a legacy.

- I give myself permission to keep going.

- I give myself permission to fail.

- I give myself permission to get back up.

## Chapter 10

# Don't Let Your Needs Drive!
# Have A Why!
# (Don't Let Your Needs Drive Your Why!)

One of the most unproductive ways to live is on a "needs" basis. This is what creates greed, feelings of inferiority, and the lack of fulfillment. When your life is motivated by a "need", you're always searching for ways to meet that need. You're never satisfied. If that need does not get met, you will sometimes do irrational things or even hurt people. A "needs" based life is one that will ultimately become a self-centered life.

If a person gets into a relationship to satisfy a "need", there will always be frustration in that relationship. Some people get into relationships out of the need for companionship. When they feel that need is not being met, they look for other avenues to meet that need. Some get into relationships out of the need for sex. If they feel that need is not being met, they explore other options. Oftentimes, that's the cause of unfaithfulness, the relationship is built on need.

### I Need A Job

I hear a lot of people say, "I need a job" or "I need a better job." What they are saying is, "I need money." The need for money drives people to be on the constant search. I see people get jobs, talk about how much they love the new job and then in a few months they are on the search again. Why? It's because they are living based on need. Living based on need is the primary cause of burnout. You get burnt out from chasing something that is always elusive. Needs are temporary. They come and go.

## What Happens When The NEEDS Change?

The number one reason why you can't be driven by need is because, at some point, that need is going to change. As you get older, your needs change. As you acquire more things, your needs change. If you lose certain things, your needs change. That's why I say they are elusive. You can't trust your needs. So that leads us to the topic at hand. You can't be driven by your need; you must be driven by your WHY!

Your "Why" is always stronger than your need. When you have a "why" your needs become less relevant. What I mean by that is when your "need" is not being met your "WHY" keeps you committed.

Let me define "why". "Why" is the bigger picture. Activity is what, but "why" is the reason. "Why" gives meaning and substance. "Why" is not an emotion but it can invoke emotion. "Needs" are about you, but your "why" is about the people you care about. In my favorite book, the Bible, it says you should 'think higher of others than you do of yourself.' That's what will make you act. It will cause you to want to meet someone's needs before your own.

The "why" is the force greater than you that fuels you to function at a level that surpasses human logic. When you have a reason, you fight for your dream. You fight for your relationship. You fight for your destiny. You fight for your legacy. "Needs" are temporary, "why" is eternal and internal. Let me explain that statement.

When Martin Luther King Jr. marched on Washington and organized various boycotts. he didn't do it to meet a need. He did it because he had a dream. He had a "why".

"I have a dream that one day little black boys and girls will be holding hands with little white boys and girls." ~ Martin Luther King Jr.

That was his "why" Even though he's gone, his "why" is still alive. His "why" kept him marching when all odds were against him. "Needs" see obstacles. "Why" only sees opportunity.

"Needs" are motivated by the present circumstance. "Why" creates a desired future that will live beyond you.

Anyone can tell you what you need but only you can define your why. Why comes from within. It's something that you're willing to give up everything for. It's something you are willing to go through pain for. It's something that no one will quite understand but you.

For some people, their "why" are their children. For some, their "why" is their parents that have gotten up in age. For others, it's seeing the poverty of a third world country. Whatever your "why" is, let that be the reason you wake in the morning. Let that be the reason you work as hard as you do. This will give purpose to your pain. This will give purpose to your day. This will give you a reason to be obsessed with getting results.

If you don't know "why", let me give you some keys to discover it. If you don't know "why", you will always live in a place of wandering.

*Here are some things to think about in discovering why.*

- Take a moment to think about what or who really means a lot to you. How would you feel if something happened or didn't happen with those people or things?

- What or who captivates your thoughts in a positive way? It could be a spouse or kids. Maybe for someone, it's your nephews or nieces. If you get the results that you desire, what does that mean for them?

- How do you want to be remembered? What mark do you want to leave on the world?

- Here is the last one, but it's the hardest sometimes to think about. What or who are you willing to give your life for?

When you start answering these questions. you will start building your "why". You will start developing a motivation that goes beyond you.

# Chapter 11

# The Five Star Life

I'm sure you're wondering what is the Five-star life? Most people have heard of the five-star hotel. That's the cream of the crop if you will. It's the top of the line. It is oftentimes defined as the "best there is". When we go on vacation, that's where we want to stay, in five-star. If you want your kids to have the best day-care, you look for the five-star day-care. If you want to eat a high-class meal, you look for the five-star restaurant. The five-star option is set apart.

It's unique in its space. It's five-star because there is nothing else that can compare. There may be 100 hotels on one street, but the five-star hotels are the ones that stand out. They are the ones that everyone dreams of spending their time in. Not only do they want to stay there, but they will also pay whatever they have to pay to stay there.

This is one of the most important principles that I have learned from people that have created amazing results in life. They learn how to live a five-star life. This is where you recognize your value and operate on a daily basis based on that discovery. This five-star life is what will make you stand out from the crowd. It's what will cause people to want to be a part of what you are doing. If you want to attract better, you must become better. If you want to attract the people that can invest in you, you must display why that investment would be a benefit to their lives or the world around you.

Let's look at what we can learn from the Hotel Market. What makes a Five-Star Hotel? I believe that this could help us position our lives to become highly productive and influential.

These are simply some of the things that I learned that can help you create a nice "five-star" life.

**Consistency Is King.**

One of the things that make you "less attractive" to people that have the ability and resources to take you to the next level is inconsistency. There is a saying that says, "A double minded man is unstable in all his ways." (James 1:8) If you're not consistent then, you can't be trusted. Most times, when you don't get where you need to be it's because of the lack of consistency.

**Protect your Space.**

Five-star neighborhoods are usually gated. There is often a gate around five-star hotels. I've even seen five-star restaurants that are gated. If you want to live a five-star life, you must protect your space. This doesn't mean live paranoid, but you understand your value. Only allow authorized people into your space. This will protect your emotions, your time, your money and so many more things that are valuable to you. Protect your space.

**Discover Your Value Expression.**

The reason that a five-star establishment can charge three times, and maybe ten times more, than other establishments in the same industry is because they know their value. They know not everyone is going to come but they know that the right people will show up. In other words, knowing your value, and being able to clearly articulate that value, is key to attracting the right people into your life. It is the key to attracting the money that you need to fulfill your mission.

**Make Excellence Your Habit.**

In everything you do, do it with everything you've got. Excellence is attractive. If you want to be viewed as someone of value, you should present yourself that way. Now, I'm not talking about going out and spending money on clothes that you can't afford. I'm talking about you being the best version of you. Dressing the best that you can. You are a professional at whatever you do. You should present yourself that way.

On my last trip to Orlando, the seminar I attended was held at the Ritz Carlton. It's a very prestigious hotel and the experience was amazing! It left a lasting impression on my mind. It made me want to come back and spend more time there, even bring my family. Why? Because of all those four points. Everyone that worked there was dressed eloquently, the grass was finely manicured, and every detail was on point. I believe that is how we should live our lives.

You should have a profound impact on the lives of the people that you meet. When you are networking and meeting new business clients or connections, you must present yourself as a five-star person. Your organization is a five-star organization. When you present yourself this way, people will tell others about you and the service you have to offer. As you can see, the five-star hotel is more than an overnight stay, it's about an experience. What type of experience are people having when they meet you? What are you giving them that, when they leave your presence, they will never forget?

You want people to talk about you, but not only that, you want them to tell others about the amazing experience they had when they met you. That's what impact is all about. You should become "THAT PERSON". What I mean by "that person" is that when they think of what you do, do they think of your name only? Five-star hotels want you to become an elite member of their hotel chain. They want you to think of them every time you think about a vacation or a business trip.

This is the key to making every networking event the most profitable and productive time that you invest. People don't care about your business card. They care about what you can do for them. They care about what experience they are going to have with you. Give them a five-star experience.

Nothing less.

## Love At First Sight

One question I get asked a lot is, "do I believe in love at first sight?" Honestly, I don't quite believe it, however what I can say is that you can make such an impression, at first sight, that others will want to know more about you. I also know that you can do the total opposite. My son and I stayed at a hotel when he ran track at the Junior Olympics. There were so many people in the city that every hotel was booked. Unfortunately, I waited until the very last minute to get a room, which resulted in us staying in, what seemed to be, a 1-1/2 star hotel. That was my first, and last time, I ever wanted to be in that atmosphere.

With the presence of social media and the myriad of ways to distribute information, you want to make sure that you are five-star ready, when you walk out the house. This could be the difference in you being stuck in the "now" or you having an opportunity that brings you into your "next."

It's time to upgrade to the Five-Star Life!

# Chapter 12

# Declutter

~~~∿⸎∿~~~

Holding on to things that no longer matter or have no purpose in your life, could be one of the most devastating things to your progress. It's funny that, while I'm writing this book, my wife and I have been having the conversation about decluttering our lives. And last year, a good friend of mine sent me a message saying it was "time to declutter before the New Year". I looked in my closet and realized that there are major issues of clutter. If I don't get rid of things, I won't have room for anything new or better to come in. Knowing when it's time to declutter is of the utmost importance.

**You Can't Hold On To That**

• One thing I learned is that there often is often an emotional attachment to certain things in our life. There are things that we know we don't need any more but because there is some type of memory attached to it, we just hold on. When I looked in my closet, I had to ask myself an important question?

**What purpose does this serve me?**

If I couldn't answer that question, I knew that it was something that didn't need to go into my "next". It was keeping me in my past. There were things like shirts that my dad, who passed away, bought for me. I didn't want to let them go but I had to realize that I had been holding on to those things for years and hadn't even worn them. That means that, at this point, there was no purpose. There are things in our lives that we hold on to that really have no purpose in our lives. It's important to identify those things, so that you can get rid of them and replace them with what you need to fulfill your purpose now.

Something else I noticed was that some of my clothes didn't even fit anymore. For the record, not because I have gained weight but because I have lost over forty pounds. I just wanted to clarify that the clothes were too big. What does that mean? It means that they no longer have a purpose for me.

There are some things that you have held onto that don't fit anymore. They don't fit the new you. Maybe who you used to be but for where you are going, they just don't fit. It hurts to keep trying to wear something that's too tight or trying to make something work that's too loose. It just doesn't work, and it creates unnecessary problems.

There are people in your life that don't fit. There are places in your life that don't fit. There are positions in your life that don't fit. There are emotions in your life that don't fit. There are attitudes in your life that don't fit. There are fears in your life that don't fit.

You must get rid of those things. If not, you will never make room. I'm not saying it's easy. I'm saying it's necessary. To get to the "next" you have to be willing to let go of the "now". Yes, you maximize the now! You take full advantage of the now, but you are going to have to eventually let go to go further faster.

**Too Much To Carry.**

For the first time this year, I flew with only one bag. I put all my clothes and everything I needed in one bag. A carry on. I realized that most of the time, when I pack for a trip, I don't even wear all the clothes that I pack. So, I decided to just bring what I needed and see how that worked out.

**Here is what I discovered.**

It took less time to get to my gate for departure. Here's why. I didn't have to stand in the line and wait to check in my baggage. I was able to go right to the security check because I already had my pre-boarding pass. I realized that what slows us down, most of the time, is that we must stop and make sure we have all our baggage with us. We don't want to leave anything behind so we're willing to spend more time waiting, to ensure that everything from our old "location" can come with us to our new "location." I missed a flight once because my baggage was too heavy, and it was beginning to cost more to fly than what I'd planned.

Here is the question....

What is it costing you to bring your baggage to your next destination? You can't come into entrepreneurship with employee baggage. It will always weigh you down and stop you from making the progress you need to make. I saw on the internet, a few weeks ago, a picture of a popular boxer as he got off his private jet in Paris, and the caption read, "no bags, I hope, when I get there."

When you arrive at your next level, that's how you should arrive "No bags." Make room for everything that this new season has for you.

# Chapter 13

# The BIG MO

IF you don't know what "The Big Mo" is let me tell you. It is what I will call the "superpower" that can move your life, business, and family to levels that you could only imagine. It can be unpredictable, sometimes. You just hit a vein and there it is, everything catapults. You start to win big. You can't really explain it. That's "The Big Mo", better known as momentum.

Everyone wants to find their stride in life, relationships, and business. "The Big Mo" is unpredictable in timing but there are some things that can be done that can generate it. I believe that momentum comes in the preparation stage of anything that you do. In this chapter, we are going to talk about ways that you can put yourself in a position to receive, when that momentum comes. It's very possible to experience momentum and lose momentum at the same time. That can happen from the lack of preparation and purpose.

Before we get into how to generate and maintain momentum, let's take a deeper look into momentum.

Momentum is aggressive, forward progress. It is a "moment of advantage". Sir Isaac Newton said, that "an object in motion stays in motion until another force interrupts that motion." Momentum is in effect until something happens that interrupts that motion. Sports teams love when momentum is on their side. It seems like they can't be touched. They can't miss a shot. They are scoring at will. The opponents just don't seem to have a chance. The coach that doesn't have the momentum has to figure out something that will interrupt that forward movement. In many cases they will call a timeout. The goal is to stop the "Big Mo."

This is what happens in our progress. Those times that we get the "Big Mo" on our side, is when life hits. As I'm typing this right now, the world is in a major pandemic. The whole world was shut down. A lot of people started the year with great momentum and the force of the pandemic slowed them down. They lost momentum. Maybe you've found yourself in that boat.

I must admit, there are some areas of my life that came to a halt during this time. It was like that "time out" the opposing coach takes to stop momentum. The "time out", or should I say adversity, is not the time to rest and allow that momentum to dissipate. That is time to plan, prepare, and execute so that you can lean into that momentum.

**The Law of The Lean**

Several years ago, my son started running track for a summer track club. His main event is high jump, but this track club recognized he had a gift for running the 4X4. Now, he didn't want to run at all. As a matter of fact, he despised running. Against his will, he eventually accepted and joined the 4X4 team. The team became good. They were so good, they qualified for the Junior Olympics.

When we got to the Junior Olympics, there were teams from everywhere. The way it looked; we didn't have a chance. It was time for our team to race, and there was a team from Houston, Texas that was on fire. They were the team that was slated to win, by far. As the race began, our team was in last place, and I mean last! And honestly, it was sad.

My son ran the Fourth leg. If you understand anything about track, that means you are the anchor. You've got a lot of responsibility. It was finally time to pass the baton to my son. Honestly, I'm thinking "just finish the race! At least we made it here." When he got the baton, something amazing and unexpected started happening.

Something hit him that I'd never seen before. It was like a nitro booster hit him. He started to catch up and, before we knew it, he was right there running with the pack. Suddenly, he is neck and neck with the leader. Now they are fighting for first and second place. As they were approaching the finish line, my son did something that was mind-blowing. He got to the finish line, leaned forward with everything he had and wouldn't you know it, they won the race.

That's when I immediately thought about the "law of the lean." His momentum and his lean caused him to go forward with a speed and impact that couldn't be stopped. This law is not only something that track athletes use to win the race, it works for every area of life, relationships, and business. This is a law that everyone needs to know and fully understand. As I studied this concept, and learned more about momentum and forward progress, I came up with the definition for "lean in" or the "law of the lean."

The "Law of the lean" is the process of recognizing and maximizing seasons of forward momentum with intentionality and precision for the purpose of accelerated progress.

This is so important to understand. Momentum, in your life or your organization, is in one of three phases.

1. Moments
2. Opportunities
3. Assignments

Moments are unexpected. You must know how to discern when you have come to a defining moment. These are the things that show up in your life and can literally change the course of your life forever. It could take your business from falling apart to becoming the most productive season you've ever seen. There have been moments in my ministry that have come and produced a season of major momentum. These moments could be centered around social events. They could be centered around a problem you discover a solution for. Painful life events can sometimes become defining moments that set the course of your destiny.

Opportunities are like doors that open for us, granting access to the NEXT. I mentioned in a previous chapter, a statement I heard that says, "every opportunity of a lifetime must be seized within the lifetime of the opportunity." I've also heard it said that "opportunities never go away, they just go to the one that takes advantage of the opportunity." So many people miss opportunities. Most of the time it's because of the lack of trust in people and in ourselves. I often wonder how many people have missed out on things that could have caused momentum to swing their way, because of scepticism. The Bible says, "your gift will make room for you." (Proverbs 18:16)

In other words, your gift will open opportunities. Getting you there, is up to God. What you do with that, is up to you. Everyone has an assignment. This is your life's work. Your assignment is why you are here on the Earth. It's important to note that assignments are continuous and progressive. This means that you may complete one assignment and discover there is something new that you've become passionate about.

At one point in my life, my assignment was to lead worship at church. That changed to pastoring a church and I'm aware that it will continue to progress. If you try to force an assignment, whose term or time has ended, it will create burnout. So, to generate new momentum, you must find the NEXT assignment.

These three phases, in the seasons of life, require that you understand when to lean in. When a defining moment comes, you must lean in. When an opportunity arises, you must lean in. When you discover an assignment, you must lean in.

**How you handle seasons of momentum will determine your rate of success.**

Everything we're talking about revolves around one statement that I heard consistently, while working in the network marketing industry.

**"New Solves All"**

I constantly heard that statement, while we were building our nutrition business. We were taught that anytime you are starting to lose momentum, you need something new to happen. It could be new prospects, a new promotion, a new event, etc. The bottom line is that new sparks something inside of you that makes you move forward with the "BIG MO". I've seen teams try something new out on the field that caused them to generate the "Big Mo". I've seen businesses start a new marketing campaign to generate the "Big Mo". I've seen churches start a new outreach program that generates the "Big Mo." Even today, I still believe that...

**"New Solves All."**

Even in your relationships, there are those moments when you need to have a new experience, such as going somewhere that you've never been. Let's look at timing. It's important to recognize when it's time to bring in something new. The best example I've seen in understanding "timing" is found in what is known as the S-Curve, or Bell Curve.

People

Entertainment

Social Media

Diet

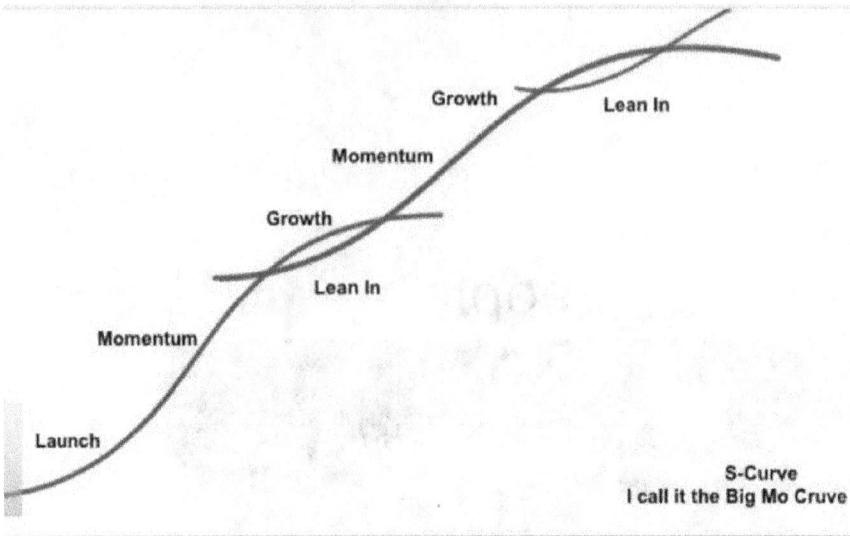

Growth

Lean In

Momentum

Growth

Lean In

Momentum

Launch

S-Curve
I call it the Big Mo Cruve

Notice in the diagram, the moment there is a plateau, there is a "lean in." Something new is introduced so that the growth and progress will continue. This is where you get more intentional and intense. If you do this correctly, you will see new momentum, which ultimately equals new growth.

Your NEXT level is always generated in your "now" activity. What you do today will determine if your next is stagnate or if your next is full of forward momentum. We all need the "Big Mo." It is God's gift to your life and purpose. Most of the time, companies phase out, people grow weary, relationships fail, and money is lost, all because we didn't recognize the season we were in, in order to maximize the momentum, we were gifted with.

If you are in a place where you feel like what you're doing is falling apart or may never work, I would invite you to look deep within and pray to God for one idea that will generate the "Big Mo." Look for the moments, opportunities, and the assignments that will catapult you forward and change the whole game for you.

**The BIG MO is on your side. Now it's time to LEAN IN!**

# Chapter 14

# The Power Of Frustration

E very visionary has a season of frustration. It could be because you know that there is more that you could be doing. It could be because you can't seem to get your team moving forward. It could be because your family is not where you know they should be. If you are a dreamer, of any sort, you are going to be frustrated. For most of us, we were taught that frustration is a bad thing. I don't believe that. I believe it is a good thing. Frustration is the gateway to your NEXT.

The frustration of your job is what was needed for you to begin to pursue your business. Oftentimes, the frustration with your kids inspires you to look for new and innovative ways to connect with them. Frustration in marriage could cause you to look for ways to spice up the marriage. The problem is that somehow frustration has been interpreted as, it's time to quit. That's so far from the truth. Sometimes we are looking for an answer from God and that answer is in your frustration. That's God saying, "it's time to make a change." It's what one writer calls "Holy Discontent." There's something on the inside of you that says, "there's got to be more than this."

Have you been there before? Maybe you're there now. Frustration is a result of something that is unresolved, unfinished, or unrealized. Frustration is neither good nor bad. It is neutral, but how you respond to that frustration is the issue. I like to look at frustration as a call that needs to be answered. IF you want to constantly progress in your life, you must learn how to 'answer the call' of frustration.

There are two responses that you can have to frustration.

1. You can respond with pessimism.
2. You can respond with optimism.

If you respond with pessimism, when you find yourself in a frustrated season, you will see it as an obstacle. If you respond with optimism, you will see it as an opportunity. Pessimism causes you to subconsciously look for reasons why things will not change. It's easy to find things that validate your negative thoughts. It's easy to find reasons why your excuses are real.

You may say, "I can't get out of this situation because I don't have enough money." The more you think that's the case, the more real that becomes to you. Optimistic people will never say "I don't have enough." They will always look for possibilities. Optimism has the opposite, subconscious effect. Your mind starts looking for a way to make it possible.

The very essence of the "law of attraction" is that, as your thoughts are directed towards a specific thing, you start to search for what you're thinking about. Next thing you know, you begin to possess the thing of your most directed thoughts.

There are three things that are required to turn frustration into the NEXT level of success.

1. New Information
2. Fresh Revelation
3. Clear Instruction

## New Information

If you're frustrated with your current situation, that means that you need to hear something different than what you've been hearing. The Bible says that "faith comes by hearing." (Romans 10:17) If that is true, and I believe it is, then fear also comes by what you hear. In times of frustration, if you are hearing negative information, or even old information, it will keep you stuck in that place of frustration.

New information gives you a new perspective. In the age that we live in, information is everywhere. There is a book, blog, or coach that can download new information that will pull you out of the place that you have found yourself in and give you the fuel you need to see massive change in your life.

## Fresh Revelation

Let me define revelation. If you are in the church world, you may have all kinds of thoughts about the word revelation. To make this simple, we'll use a simple working definition. Revelation is the 'uncovering of something that always was but, for whatever reason, you've never noticed it'. That's important to note.

It's not something that doesn't exist. You just missed it. Oftentimes, there is just one thing that we are missing that will get us to the place we desire. Revelation comes from searching in places that you've never looked before. Your breakthrough is right there in front of you. Open your eyes and think. There is a concept or an idea that will change the game for you.

## Clear Instruction

I have heard it said that "you are one instruction away from the best days of your life." The truth is, the "NEXT" is oftentimes hidden in the last instruction you didn't follow. The reason many of us are so unclear, in what we should be doing, is because we are listening to instructions that are not congruent with our vision.

If you are looking to be an entrepreneur, you can't get coached by an employment specialist. This is what many of us do. We ask advice from those who have never done what we're desiring to do. Truth is that their thoughts don't matter. They are not on the same frequency as you.

Clear instruction only comes from someone that has been where you are going. You can't get clear instruction from the experts on the news stations. In my opinion, they are only experts at negativity. The right instruction could be the very thing that unlocks your greatness and catapults your destiny.

I believe that if you are missing any of these three elements, you will live your life in a place of absolute frustration. It's easy to get stuck in old information or even in an old story that you continually repeat to yourself. Fresh revelation comes to open our eyes to possibilities never thought of. Your answer, in a lot of cases, will be found there. And lastly, as you obtain clear instruction, let what has been frustrating you be the thing that launches you!

# Chapter 15

# What's On Your Mind

Ond day I decided to open my Facebook and scroll, like we do. I noticed, on the FB home page, a question in the status box that really made me think. I've seen it so many times but this time it hit me differently. I'm not sure why, but it did. The question was "what's on your mind?" This time it made me take a step back and evaluate the question. I logged off Facebook and took some time to intentionally ponder what was really 'on my mind'.

I think this is a question that everyone should consider. It may be one of the most important questions that you can ask yourself. Whatever is on your mind, will eventually be what's in your hand. That's why this is such a vital question. It is so true that "you are what you think you are" (Proverbs 23:7). Of course, the Bible says, "as a man thinks in his heart so is he." What this means is that we must fix what is on our mind if we want to see change. High achievers think differently. High-capacity leaders think differently. People who are producing at high levels think differently. That is really the only thing that separates the average from the extraordinary.

### What Is Mindset?

A fixed mental attitude or disposition that predetermines a person's responses to and interpretations of situations. – (thefreedictionary)

The part of this definition that stands out to me is "predetermined responses to and interpretations of situations". In other words, our responses to situations are already predetermined. For example, if you're leading a company, how you handle a setback is predetermined by your mindset. How you respond to your spouse in stressful situations is already predetermined. How you interpret life around you is predetermined. This is good news.

It's good news because if your mindset predetermines your responses and interpretation, then how you respond and interpret can be changed by changing your mindset. I believe this is why the Apostle Paul said, "Be not conformed to this world but be transformed by the renewing of the mind." (Romans 12:2) Transformation is always connected to changing the way you think.

If you are like me, you've heard this, pretty much all your life, that you must change your thinking. You've heard "change your mind, change your life." One day, while listening to an incredible sermon on "capturing your thoughts", something dawned on me. The preacher was discussing the importance of thinking better thoughts and changing your mindset, and it made me realize that we talk a lot about what needs to happen with our mind but very little about how.

I've concluded that most of us know that we need to change our thoughts, but we just don't know how. In discovering this as the problem, I went on a search to find out the solution of "how". What I found is that shifting your mindset is a process. There are steps that you must go through to interrupt negative thought patterns so that you can get to, what I will call, the "mindset of manifestation".

What I found is that there are four stages to shifting your mindset. We're going to walk through these four stages, to help you shift into the "mindset of manifestation". This could be one of the most important things that I have ever discovered, and it has literally changed the very course of my life. Pay close attention to the next several chapters. There will be some specific instructions that will be paramount in reconstructing your mindset.

# Chapter 16

# Reprogram Your Mind

❧

Everyone came into the world with a 'clean slate' or a 'flexible mindset'. I touched the surface of this in chapter three, dealing with childlike belief. Our mindset is formed over the course of time, and we are conditioned, or programmed, with certain thought patterns.

The more we experience life, the more it programs our mind. Just like a computer, sometimes we must reprogram our mind so that we can function at maximum capacity. I remember one time my computer got stuck on the start menu, when I turned it on. I had to take it to the computer store to have it checked out.

They found that my computer needed a new hard drive because my hard drive had become corrupted. This is what I believe we need, at times. We need a new hard drive. That's what we are going to do. We are going to install a new hard drive. I'm going to call this the "NEXT level hard drive". I hope you're ready, this is going to take a little intentionality. The first thing we're going to do is get rid of the old hard drive because we all have had some negative thought patterns that have held us back and caused us to hold on to self-limiting beliefs.

**Here's The Strategy:**

Take some time to think about the negative words you've held on to, from others, that have become a part of your thought process. Some of these words or thoughts are things that you've spoken about yourself as well. This is the very practice I've used personally, and to help others reprogram their thoughts about themselves.

In the section below, write down negative words that have become thought patterns:

Example (my 10th grade teacher said I would never be anything).

_____

_____

_____

_____

_____

_____

_____

_____

Now that you have done that we are going to "reverse engineer" this thought. We must delete that file that has been there for years, maybe since your childhood. The ancient writer gave us a principle that is very vital in this process.

Here is what he said,

*"Brothers and sisters, I do not consider myself yet to have taken hold of it. But one thing I do: Forgetting what is behind and straining toward what is ahead,"*
(Philippians 3:13)
~ Apostle Paul

He said that he "forgot what is behind him and strain or press towards what is ahead". This is what is called "delete and replace". So now let's replace that negative idea that you had about yourself.

Write a replacement statement. In my example, I said my 10th grade teacher said I would never be anything. (True story, by the way).

My replacement statement is "I am more than enough to accomplish everything that I pursue, and I will walk in purpose and reach massive levels of success."

This will be one of the statements that you will write every morning and say it out loud. This will reprogram your unconscious mind. Before you know it, that old thought or idea will no longer have power. You are literally putting that behind you and pressing towards a higher goal.

**Reprogram Statement:**

_____
_____
_____
_____
_____
_____
_____
_____

Remember, get a notebook, and write this every day and say it out loud.

# Chapter 17

# Reframe Your Mind

W e dealt with the mental programming, now we have to deal with your mental framework. Framework is the structure of ideas. I like to say, it is the habits and environments that make up your mindset. Everyone has a mental framework. Everyone has habits and environments that we find ourselves in that keep us in certain thought structures.

My dad was an artist. He painted some of the most amazing oil paintings of the Buffalo Soldiers, Native Americans, and African art. I remember one time he went out and got the most expensive frame for one of his pictures. I asked him why he got that frame. There were a lot of frames that were cheaper. He said, "because this frame will give the painting more protection and it will be more valuable when I take it to the art show".

Therefore, the frame around your mindset is important. It will protect your thoughts. It will keep you from allowing negativity or corrupt files from coming in. Let's look at some frames that surround our minds that could be causing us to be stuck in limiting thoughts or causing our programming to go bad. On the next few pages, we will review some negative "frames" and show you some more productive "frames" to cover your mind. This will protect your thoughts and make them more valuable for you.

This is the 'basic frame' for most peoples' lives. As you can see at the top of this frame are people. I will never forget when I heard someone say, "show me the people that you hang around, and I will show you your future." No one influences your way of thinking more than the people you are around the most.

When my wife and I decided that we were ready to break the financial barriers we had in our mind, we found people that had the type of money we desired and got around them. This was changing the framework of our thought process concerning money.

We immediately noticed that our conversation changed. We noticed that our activity changed. This was something that we are very intentional about. We will fly from Oklahoma to South Florida, just to get around others who speak differently about money, so that it will stretch our minds and "frames". I know you've heard it before but it's vital that you consider the people that you have been around. Are they adding to your destructive thoughts or are they creating in you a thought process of progress and purpose?

This is important, no matter what space you're in. If you are in business, be careful of the other business owners you are around. If their conversation is about how bad business is, RUN! If you are a pastor and you are around other pastors that are talking about how bad pastoring is, RUN! If you are a parent and other parents are talking about how difficult it is to parent, RUN! Find the people that are speaking a language of productivity.
Social media is one of the greatest, and most powerful, inventions that we have ever seen, with most of the world on some social media platform. It is great, in the sense that it keeps us connected, on some level, however it creates a 'frame' in our minds that causes us to compare.

A lot of that comparison is unconscious, and it will hit you at strange times. You will be doing just fine and then suddenly, you will start thinking about someone else's business, someone's look, or someone else's relationship. That's where the deadly sin of comparison starts.
I always say that it's very dangerous to compare yourself to someone else's "highlight reel". Comparison has three levels, and they are all equally dangerous.

1. You compare yourself to people that seem to be doing better than you.
2. You compare yourself to people that seem to be on the same level.
3. You compare yourself to people that seem to be doing worse than you.

Social Media has a way of pulling you into one of these places.

The first one causes you to feel less than because you're always thinking these people are better than you. The second one causes you to say "well, I'm doing just as good as they are". The third one causes you to say "well, at least I'm doing better than they are."

My thought, on the subject, is that you must define a clear purpose as to why you want to be on social media. Is it for marketing? Is it for connection? Is it to keep people updated on your life happenings? Is it for inspiring and empowering people?

Dr. Myles Monroe says, "Where purpose is not known, abuse is inevitable." If there is no purpose to your social media activity, it will become a negative frame. Not only that, but it will consume all your mental space and time.

The second "frame" I want to discuss is diet. I know you're asking, "what does my diet have to do with anything?" It has a lot to do with it. Many studies have proven that certain foods will affect how you think. It will affect your memory. It will affect your focus. I'm not going to spend a lot of time on this one but what I will tell you is that if you're eating a lot of fast-food, greasy foods or a lot of sugars, it is affecting how your mind works.

Healthier foods will always equal healthier thinking. Think about it. After that big Thanksgiving meal, what happens? You feel lethargic. You can't think straight. That would be one of the worst times to make a major decision. The problem is a lot of people eat horrible food all day and then try to make major life decisions, and it just doesn't work.

We eat horrible food and say "now, I'm ready to conquer the world!". It doesn't work. Your diet is a vital part of your mental framework. Create a good habit of eating better and you will see a great habit of thinking better.

The last "frame" I'll discuss is the environment. Your environment is vital to your mindset. If you are always in a stressful, high pressure or hostile environment, it will contaminate your mindset. That's why if someone works in a very hostile workplace, they can bring that 'environment' into their home. I've talked to so many couples that have said, "As soon as he/she started working that job, it went downhill from there." What they are saying is, as soon as they got into that environment, their mindset changed. How they respond changed. Their mood changed. They get angry easier, or they're worn out all the time. That type of environment is toxic to your thought life.

One of the master keys to success is to find environments that feed your potential and elevate your mindset. As I stated previously, there are times that my wife and I will fly miles away, just to get in environments that will stretch us and cause us to think higher. If you are constantly in an environment that brings you down, that is not the place for you. Every environment either drains or fuels you. The truth is a lot of our mental conditioning is a result of where we have spent our time. If you are going to recondition your mindset, you must be intentional about your environment.

# Chapter 18

# Re-Image Your Mind

O ne of the most powerful, God-given tools that we have is our imagination. Imagination is the way that we see beyond our current reality. It is the way that we see possibilities.

Imagination is the root of vision. In other words, you always imagine something first, and then what you've imagined becomes the vision you begin to pursue.

**So, what is imagination?**

According to Oxford Dictionaries, "it is the faculty or action of forming new ideas, or images or concepts of external objects not present to the senses."

Here's how powerful imagination is. I want you to think about a horse, that is purple, running through a river, while a bear rides it. I know that was a very silly analogy, but I also know that you started picturing in your mind the image of a purple horse with a bear riding on it, running through the river. That's how your imagination works. It can literally formulate any image that it is told to form.

Imagination always leads to a desire. Your desire always leads to action. Therefore, mastering the imagination is vital. There was an old classic song by The Temptations entitled, "Just my Imagination". The chorus was "Just my imagination, running away with me."

The whole concept of the song was interesting when I read the lyrics. I heard the song but never really listened to what it was saying. The concept was that he had a girl that he could see himself with. He could see himself marrying her, but it was just in the imagination. Here is one of the lines in the song.

Soon we'll be married

And raise a family, whoa yeah

A cozy, little home out in the country

With two children, maybe three

I tell you I can visualize it all

This couldn't be a dream for too real it all seems

But it was just my imagination, once again running away with me

I tell you it was just my imagination running away with me

While this is a hit song from the 70's, it speaks so much to the truth of how our imaginations work. You can literally imagine and visualize anything. The root word for imagination is the word "image." Now let's define "image." Webster's Dictionary defines "image" as a "visual representation of something: a mental picture or impression of something." Everyone has a mental image of three different areas.

1. An image of the world.
2. An image of people.
3. An image of you.

These three areas are the foundations of your greatest imaginations. How you view the world, people, and your personal image will determine the images you have in your mind which, in turn, forms your imaginations.

## The World Image

You may have heard this referred to as "world view". Either way it goes, it's how you see the world around you. If you believe that the world is a terrible place to live in and that everything in the world is against you, then that will be how you receive from the world. I hear people say that "the world is going to hell in a handbasket" or that 'the world is just getting worse and worse."
As I stated previously, as I write, we are in the midst of one of the worst pandemics we've seen in recent history. It has been an economic disaster for so many people. I am, right now, in the midst of so much fear and panic. But I've seen another side of this. There is a select group of people that have prospered in ways that are mind blowing. I have seen some entrepreneurs' businesses double, and even triple. I've watched people make some major pivots that have shaped their business forever.

I asked myself a critical question, as I noticed the vast difference between those that are panicking and those that are prospering. The difference that was most evident, was the image they had of the world. Those that were prospering didn't see this time as the end of the world. They saw it as an opportunity. They saw it as a moment to expand their business.

When everything shut down, they figured out how to leverage the internet to increase their influence. On the contrary, some people said, "well I guess it's over. We tried." They closed their doors and just accept things as they were.

One group's imagination was that of panic and fear. They could only imagine everything going horribly wrong. They could only visualize their business crashing and falling apart. The other group could only imagine that this would be the moment they have been waiting on. They began to visualize more customers and more clients.

During this time of chaos, my wife and I had the most prosperous year of our lives. Our church experienced massive growth, during a time when so many businesses and organizations were going bankrupt. Again, the difference was the image we had of the world.

What is the image you have held on to, of the world, that could be blocking you from moving into the best days of your life? Is the world a horrible place to live in or is it a place of massive opportunity that is waiting on you to show up? This could be the difference between you just "living" and you making a life with legacy.

## The Image of People

This is a big one. Relationships are the currency of life and how you view relationships can detrimentally affect how far you go in life. If you think that everyone is a "hater" or that everyone is out to get you, then that is going to become your greatest stumbling block. Now, I understand that all of us have been let down by people. I understand that you have some bad deals. I've entered some bad business deals myself, some ministry partnerships that turned out horrible, but I can't allow the image I form of people to become negative or skewed.

Too many people live in a place of suspicion. I've heard Andy Stanley talk about Suspicion vs Trust. If you start your relationship with suspicion, then you will never be able to build a solid relationship. The foundation of any relationship must be trust. The way we start is that trust has to be earned, but some have the idea that until then, they'll just be suspicious. The problem is that it's hard to grow in trust.

What has to happen is that you have to find out what "images" you have of people and why. In many cases, the trauma, or even drama, in our lives has caused us to categorize people. If someone wants to partner in business and we've had someone 'do us wrong' in the past, we could unconsciously put this new person in the same category as the person that did us wrong. One way to know if you are doing this is by the language you use. If you say, "All business partnerships end up messy." That is an indication that you have categorized.

Another indicator is that you begin associating what someone else did or said with the new relationship you're trying to build. "I've heard this before" can mean that you are building from the foundation of suspicion. I've sat across from married couples in counselling sessions and heard one spouse say, "my ex used to do that." That means that you are in a new marriage with an old image.

To get rid of those old images you've held on to of people that did you wrong, I want to invite you to follow these steps:

1.  Forgive. Yes, forgiveness is going to be a master key. Forgiveness is never for the other person. Forgiveness is always for you. When you hold on to the offenses, it is only hurting your progress. Forgiveness can sometimes be very difficult, but it is extremely necessary.

2.  Take responsibility. Let me explain. You cannot control the actions of others, but you can control your response. Truth is, people are going to do things that hurt you, but you don't have to allow any of those things to affect your NEXT. You can still choose to love. You can still choose to succeed. You can still choose to treat others right.

3.  Become. What does this mean? This means that you are going to become committed to "becoming" the person that you would like to attract. If you want to attract high paying clients, you must become a high paying client. If you want to attract an amazing spouse, you must become an amazing spouse. Become what you want to attract.

**The Image Of You**

Number three, of becoming, is a great Segway into this topic of Self-Image. I wanted to put this one last because I think it is one of the greatest challenges, for many. It's a struggle for some of the greatest motivators and leaders in the world. I know major coaches that struggle with self-image. I've struggled with self-image. It is sometimes easier to believe in other people, more than you believe in yourself. Therefore, people will work hours on someone else's dream and never work a day on their own dream.

You will never, and I mean never, rise above the image you have of yourself, if you don't believe in YOU! It's hard to get the marketplace, ministry, or any entity to believe in you, if you don't believe in yourself. Procrastination is, oftentimes, rooted in low self-image. Fear is, oftentimes, rooted in low self-image. Even how you choose relationships is rooted in low self-image. If you want to elevate your life, you must elevate the image that you have of yourself.

The big question I have is where did you get the image you have of yourself? Why do you see yourself the way you do? Now, I believe that your self-image must begin with how you see God. If your self-image is formed from anywhere other than God, then it is going to be "off". I have other teachings on some of our false images of God, but I won't talk about that in this book. But if we see God as powerful, creative, loving, all-knowing, and victorious then we must start seeing ourselves the same way.

Below is a scripture from one of my favorite books in the Bible, that will bring understanding to the above statement.

Genesis 1:26 Then God said, "Let us make man in **our image**, after **our likeness**. And let them have dominion over the fish of the sea and over the birds of the heavens and over the livestock and over all the earth and over every creeping thing that creeps on the earth." (ESV)

You may be a product of your parents. You may be a product of your environment. You may be whatever race you are, but you are made in God's image. Wow! This was one of the greatest discoveries of my life. If this becomes your focus, you will elevate your image of yourself. You wouldn't think so low of God, would you?

This is the first thing you must do. Change the image you have of you so that it will change how you present yourself to the world. Remember, no matter what happens in your life, you will always default back to the image you have of yourself. If you see yourself as a product of a bad upbringing, it doesn't matter if you win a million dollars, you will revert to how you see yourself. I've seen people go from one abusive relationship to the next. The problem is not the relationship. The problem is the image that you have of yourself.

The moment you change your image, will be the moment that you change what you attract. It will change how you handle opportunities. It will change how you handle wins and losses. Changing your self-image is paramount in changing your life and taking control of your mindset.

# Chapter 19

# Renew Your Mind

R omans 12:2 states, "And do not be conformed to this world, but be transformed by the renewing of your mind, that you may prove what is that good and acceptable and perfect will of God."

I couldn't talk about renewing the mind without bringing out this scripture from the Bible. The reason this is so important to start with, is because it suggests that there is no transformation without there being a renewing of the mind.

Could it be that the reason you can't get to the next level is because you're trying to go to the next level or new level with the old mindset? I've heard it said that "the way you think won't get you there." Renewing the mind is not a onetime experience. It is a continual practice that you must have in place.

We have a lot of habits in our lives but this one should be the most important. It should be a priority. It should be non-negotiable in your life and should be just as important as eating or bathing or breathing. I believe that if you don't continually renew your mind, you are no longer "living". Of course, you may be breathing but you've stopped living, or "thriving in life".

The mind is one of the most important muscles to exercise yet, it is one of the least talked about. Most people start going to the gym to lose weight or gain muscle but never go through the continual renewal process. So, what happens is you lose weight or get in shape, but it stops there. You never go any further because you only renew your mind long enough to reach a certain goal but never go further, so that you could exceed what you never thought would be possible.

Now, I know many of you have heard about the renewing of the mind, however let me make it more practical, starting with this important statement to remember...

"Once your mind is stretched, it can never go back to where it once was."
I've heard so many speakers say this, although I'm not sure who the originator is, but the statement is the absolute truth. Renewing the mind is about stretching the mind. Making your thought process bigger and better.

If you have a smartphone, specifically an iPhone because I think that's the best way to live, you know about the updates. Just the other day, my iPhone informed me that there were updates available. This time, I decided to read the updates, since I've never actually done that before.

Here are some of the things that I learned.

1. It would fix bugs.
2. It would change the look of my screen.
3. It would fix unexpected crashes.

Those were just a few to name. It asked me if I wanted to update, which meant I had a choice. It was up to me. I realized that updates are the same as renewing the mind. So, we need constant mental updates. Think about this. If I had not updated, I would have been frustrated because my phone would not have worked at maximum capacity. I would still have sudden crashes. I would not have the new look. I would not be able to get the new features. I hope you're getting this.

There is a lot that you could be doing but maybe you didn't "accept" the latest updates. Maybe the reason that you are "crashing" is because you have not updated. There could be new software that you have rejected.

In this next section, you will see the Mind Renewal Wheel. If these tools become an integral part of your life, you will obtain continued mind renewal, growth and progressively move into your NEXT.

# Chapter 20

# The Priority Of Next

O ne of the questions that I hear most is, what's NEXT? This may be one of the most difficult things to find the answer to, especially after your life has been altered due to the loss of a job, the loss of a loved one, or some type of sudden change.

The truth is that we are always going to experience change, therefore we are always going to be faced with a "next". Truth is, the quicker you can close the gap between your current circumstance and the next thing in your life, the quicker you can see progress. So many people are stuck where they are because they have not made this most important discovery called "next".

I'll take some time to help you understand the word "next" so that we can discover how to do what I call "shift from your now to your next". "Next" is an action word. The nature of the word denotes movement or progress. It is a word that says, something has changed. Not only has something changed but something has been left behind. Making that shift will always require something to be left behind. That may be feelings, unforgiveness, bitterness, pains of your past, old relationships, the list goes on and on.

"Next" also signifies the thing that comes directly after. It is the nearest position from where you are currently. The step that must be taken to go forward or get to a desired outcome. The worst feeling in the world for any leader, business, pastor, or any type of visionary, is to know that there is something greater but not know how to get there.

I would submit to you that this is most likely one of the greatest causes of stress and maybe even depression. That feeling of "being stuck". The feeling of "being stuck" is where the feeling of failure is birthed. That is where the anxiety of life is birthed. When you are in a place and feel like you can't get out.

I read an article on Digital Hub that said "80% of Americans feel stuck in a routine". As I've said in an earlier chapter, most people are trapped in a cycle. Most of us want better for our lives and family but it's not because we're greedy, it's because we know there's more. There's more to life than getting up in the morning and going to the same place everyday trading a whole bunch of your time for a fraction of someone else's money. I believe it's time to break that cycle and find out what's next for you, so that you don't stay in that place of frustration for the rest of your life.

**What's NEXT?**

Next comes four ways:

1.  Planning. An intentional action where you decide your desired outcome and go for it. You write the vision and make it plain. Planning is the best way to get to your "next" because it's based on you and your decision. It's based on your personal passion. It's based on a dream that you desire to see fulfilled in your life.

2.  Neglect. Neglect is the worst way to enter the "next". That's because it is based on you just kind of "going with the flow of life" and hoping that everything works out for you. If you never change the oil in your car then, guaranteed, you will not move to your next destination. If you don't show up to work, you will lose your job and be forced into your "next". Neglect could be the most painful way to enter the "next" because you have to 'clean up the mess". Management is the key to avoiding neglect. If you manage life, you will never have to worry about neglect forcing you into a place you don't desire.

3. Time. Since time never stops, it will always bring about a "next". In time, things just change, and you must know how to move with it. You must know how to remain relevant and understand the times that you live in. If you want to keep moving, you must understand that the way things were done 20 years ago, will not keep you moving today. Change is inevitable.

**Here are two types of change that you want to be aware of:**

1. Evolutionary Change. This is a change that happens because of time. If you only move
   with evolutionary change, you will eventually become extinct.

2. Revolutionary Change. This is that intentional change that I talked about earlier. This is when you decide to do something that will bring you into the next level of your life. This is when a company decides to do something innovative that changes their industry. This is when you make a move that may be risky or edgy, but you go for it and change your family history.

4. Life. Sometimes this can be the most painful way to experience your "next". This could be the loss of a loved one. This could be the loss of a job. It could be a divorce. Life itself will push you into a "next". The key is to understand that there are some questions that will not be answered. With every obstacle there is a hidden opportunity. Some of the greatest movements were birthed out of the pain of loss. Some people didn't discover their "next" until something happened that created a burden to help other people.

## Think About These Stories

Mothers Against Drunk Driving was started after Candice Lightner's 13-year-old daughter was killed by a drunk driver. She took one of the most devastating things that could happen and discovered the "next" for her life.

The great football player Inky Johnson suffered a life-threatening injury that left his right arm paralyzed and ended his football career and hopes of going to the NFL. He used that tragedy to create a voice of hope to millions of people. It was through that injury that he discovered his "next".

There are many stories like those. People have lost their jobs and used it as a launching pad to start their businesses. Here is my point: your "next" comes in all types of ways but whatever happens, never stop pursuing. Never stop believing. Plans may change. Dreams may be cut short, like in the case of Inky. His NFL career was taken away but there is always something that you can pursue next.

## How do I Discover The Next?

I'm glad you asked. Well, maybe I would like to think that you would ask. Let's look at some ways to discover your "next". I believe these five things are what high-capacity leaders and world changers do to keep shifting from "now" to "next".

The first key, I believe, is exposure. Oftentimes the reason that we are stuck in one place is because we have never experienced anything else. If you never see anything greater than where you are, most likely you will never pursue anything greater than that. Exposure expands experience. It's vital to constantly get exposed to something new. Second, you should seek out new information. Third, seek out places that you've never visited. Fourth, seek out new networks of people that you have never been around. Lastly, seek out new careers that are out there. I try to make it a priority to constantly go to seminars and conferences. I make sure that I travel somewhere that I've never been. The reason is, I've learned the value of exposure.

You must choose to make getting to the "next" a priority. It must be intentional. You must realize that what's next is greater than what is. You may be in business. You may be in ministry. You may be working a job. You may have gone through a real tough time in your life. Right now, it may seem like you will never see anything better than the way it is now, but I assure you that greater is in your "NEXT". I always like to say that your greatest days are not behind you, your greatest days are not in front of you. Your greatest days are inside of you.

**Remember You Got NEXT!!!!!!!**